FIRST STEPS IN
BIBLICAL CRITICISM

Studies in Judaism

FIRST STEPS IN
BIBLICAL CRITICISM

D.R.G. Beattie

UNIVERSITY
PRESS OF
AMERICA

Lanham • New York • London

Library of Congress Cataloging-in-Publication Data

Beattie, Derek Robert George.
First steps in biblical criticism.

(Studies in Judaism)
Includes bibliographical references.
1. Bible. O.T. Daniel—Criticism, interpretation,
etc. 2. Bible. O.T.—Criticism, interpretation,
etc.—History. I. Title. II. Series.
BS1555.2.B44   1988   220.6'01   88–17119
ISBN 0–8191–7053–4 (alk. paper)

For Karen

Contents

Preface   ix

Part I

HISTORY AND PRINCIPLES

1. The need for critical study   3

2. Some stages in the development of the critical
    approach   7
    (i)   Antiquity and the Middle Ages   7
    (ii)   Early modern times   12
    (iii) The beginnings of modern biblical criticism   18
    Note on Moses and the Pentateuch   20

3. Some basic principles   25
    (i)   Source analysis   25
    (ii)   Textual criticism   32

Part II

CRITICISM IN PRACTICE: THE CASE OF DANIEL

4. The starting-point   43

5. Preliminary observations and their implications   49

6. Daniel's life and times   57

7. Daniel's future   65
    Note on ideas of chronology in antiquity   79

8.   The book of Daniel is . . .   81

Epilogue and Prospect   93

Appendices   97

Index   103

Preface

This little book has grown out of a course of lectures given to first-year students in the Queen's University, which in turn was motivated by the realization that our students, steeped from childhood in knowledge of the bible, sometimes experience some difficulty in adapting to a system of biblical study rather different to that to which they have previously been accustomed. In particular they often just do not see the need to ask critical questions and are — quite rightly — suspicious of having conclusions on such questions presented to them simply on the authority of scholars.

The course, then, and the book which stems from it, set out to demonstrate that biblical criticism is not a relatively recent phenomenon, practised by rather tiresome individuals who are intent on upsetting traditional opinions and values, but an extremely ancient practice which is inseparable from the serious study of the scriptures of two of the world's largest religious movements.

The first part illustrates, by referring to suggestions put forward at various periods, the long history of critical enquiry into the origin of the biblical books and the establishment of the correct (or best) form of their texts, and considers some of the basic principles which led to the rise of the modern science of biblical criticism. The second part offers an introduction to the study of a whole book, using as an exemplar the book of Daniel, a book which lends itself admirably, even in translation, to this purpose.

In the preparation of a book of this kind the work of many predecessors has inevitably been drawn upon. If few sources, apart from reference to primary texts, have been acknowledged, it is because my dependence on the work of others has been largely unconscious, but there is one area in particular in which I am conscious of my dependence. For my understanding of Daniel chapter 2 (pp.85ff.) I am indebted to an article by Dr P.R. Davies, "Daniel Chapter Two", in *Journal of Theological Studies*, XXVII/2 (1976) pp. 392-401. Unless otherwise indicated, biblical quotations in Part I are presented in my own translation; in Part II they are taken from *The New English Bible*, Second Edition (c) 1970 by permission of Oxford and Cambridge University Presses.

I must record my gratitude to my two colleagues, Dr Desmond Alexander and Miss Gillian Keys, who read my manuscript, spotted many errors and made various helpful suggestions. I am grateful, too, to Jacob Neusner and Ernest Frerichs for giving my work a home in their series. Most of all, I acknowledge my debt to those successive cohorts of undergraduates who, wittingly or not, have contributed greatly to the shaping of what follows.

D.R.G. Beattie

PART I

HISTORY AND PRINCIPLES

1

Chapter 1

The Need for Critical Study

The simplest answer to the question of what the bible is is that it is the name given to the collection of writings which is recognized by Jews and Christians as canonical scripture. But already in this simple statement we are using the word bible to refer to two different things, for, while Christians divide their bible into two parts or "testaments", only the first of these, the "Old Testament" of the Christians, is the bible of the Jews. If we proceed to investigate the contents of different volumes marked "bible", we find that, even leaving the New Testament out of account, the question becomes still more complex.

If we look first at a Jewish bible, we find that it contains twenty-four books arranged as in Appendix 1. It will be noted that this traditional enumeration reckons Samuel, Kings, Chronicles, and Ezra-Nehemiah together, as one book each, while the twelve minor prophets are also treated as one book. If we turn to a Christian bible from the Protestant tradition, we find the same contents but arranged in a different order and with the total now reckoned as thirty-nine, as in Appendix 2.

The reason for the difference in order is simply that the Jewish arrangement reflects the liturgical usage of Judaism which has no significance in Christianity. The Torah is read publicly and systematically Sabbath by Sabbath in the synagogue service, each weekly portion being accompanied by a reading from the Prophets. The volumes known collectively as the Writings are not used in the same way, although parts of them have liturgical uses. Many individual Psalms, for example, are read in the course of services, and the grouping together of Song of Songs, Ruth, Lamentations, Ecclesiastes and Esther reflects the fact that these five scrolls (as they are known) are read, respectively, at the festivals of Passover, Shavuot (or Pentecost), the ninth of Ab, Sukkot (Booths, or Tabernacles) and Purim. The Christian church, having no reason to preserve this arrangement, split up the Writings and placed the individual volumes of this section alongside other volumes of an apparently similar nature. Thus, the Former Prophets, now judged to

3

be historical in character, were joined by the other "historical" books, Chronicles, Ezra and Nehemiah, Ruth and Esther; Daniel was inserted amongst the Prophets, as was Lamentations, which was attached to the book of Jeremiah, its presumed author; and the poetic books which remained were placed between the "history" and "prophecy" sections.[1]

Turning again to a Roman Catholic edition of the bible, we find the same classification as in the Protestant bible, but a longer list of contents (see Appendix 3). In the historical section two books, Tobit and Judith, are inserted between Nehemiah and Esther, while two more, I & II Maccabees, follow Esther. Two new titles, Wisdom and Ecclesiasticus (sometimes called Ben Sira, or Sirach), are appended to the poetic section, while an additional prophetic book, Baruch (the sixth and final chapter of which is sometimes distinguished as the "Epistle of Jeremiah"), makes its appearance following Lamentations. A closer examination will reveal that the books of Daniel and Esther are longer than they are in the Protestant bible. If we go back to that Protestant bible for a moment, we may find all these works grouped together in a section between the Old and New Testaments — or, perhaps, in a separate volume — marked Apocrypha, along with three other books, I & II Esdras (sometimes known, rather confusingly, as III & IV Esdras)[2] and the Prayer of Manasseh, which we meet here for the first time, and four items which represent the differences between Esther and Daniel as they are presented in Catholic and Protestant editions.

If, finally, we examine a bible stemming from the Greek Orthodox church, we find a collection slightly different from any we have seen so far (see Appendix 4). This collection includes all of the contents of the Catholic bible *plus* I Esdras and the Prayer of Manasseh (both of which we found in the Protestant Apocrypha) and, in addition, a third book of Maccabees, while the book of Psalms has an extra chapter, Psalm 151.

We could roam still further afield and find, for example, that the bible of the Ethiopic church includes the book of Enoch (from which a quotation appears in Jude vv.14,15 in the New Testament) and the book of Jubilees, but already enough has been said to make the point clear. A Catholic and a Protestant, a Jew and an Orthodox Christian (to say nothing of an Ethiopic one) may each give a different answer to the question of what constitutes the bible, and each answer will be quite correct and completely satisfactory if the questioner is seeking to establish the tradition of one particular church. However, the impartial enquirer — whatever his persuasion — who seeks an objective answer to his question will recognize in these differences in content and arrangement indications that the collection of writings

4

known as the bible has had a history of its own which merits investigation and which requires for its understanding the application of reasoned judgement rather than the pronouncements of ecclesiastical authority.

The existence of different formulations of the canon points up the need for study, but even if only one collection were recognized to exist, the fact that it is a collection which includes various works of different kinds and ages would call for an enquiry into the origin of its different parts and the relationships between them. In other words, even if the study of the bible is undertaken within a denominational framework, where the existence of other traditions may be ignored, rather than from a neutral standpoint, the need arises to enquire into the nature and the origin, the authorship, the date of composition and the purpose behind the composition of the individual books. In short, the necessity for critical study is inherent in the nature of the bible.

If the need for study becomes evident on looking into the bible, it also becomes quickly apparent that the process of finding answers to the questions which necessarily arise will not be a simple one to be quickly dispatched. A decision on the origin and date of, say, the books of the prophets will not be simply a matter of locating certain individuals in history, assigning to them particular volumes and closing the enquiry. The duplication of material (e.g. Is. 2:2-4 and Mic. 4:1-3), indications of composite authorship in several books (e.g. Isaiah, Jeremiah, Zechariah) or even the sheer improbability that there could have been a prophet called Malachi[3], all suggest a more complex origin for this literature.

The study of other sections of the Old Testament we may expect to be no less straightforward. The book of Kings, for example, is full of chronological inconsistencies. Some of these may have originated through errors in copying the text in ancient times, but many may very well bear witness to the complex process by which the book was produced. Or, to take another example, the fact that one book — Samuel — should credit two different men (David in I Sam. 17; Elhanan in II Sam. 21) with the slaying of the Philistine champion Goliath indicates not only the historical problem of who actually did the deed but the literary question of how the material which includes such clearly incompatible statements arose.

There is another factor which makes critical study of the bible necessary but which may not be immediately evident to those who read the bible only in translation, although those who pay attention to the footnotes provided in many editions of the bible will gain some insight into some of the problems faced by translators. No original text, in the sense of the manuscript written by the author, exists for any part of the bible, and there may on occasion be uncertainty as to

what the author intended to say, either because something is obviously wrong with the text that has come down to us or because there is disagreement in wording between different manuscripts.

Biblical criticism (the noun is not, of course, used in its vernacular, pejorative sense) is the science which has been developed in order to find answers to the questions inherent in the bible. It is often thought of as a modern phenomenon but, while it is true that it has developed greatly in the last century or so, its beginnings are very ancient indeed. The questions which gave rise to the science — both those which relate to matters of authorship, date and purpose (the matters embraced in what 19th-century scholars called "Higher Criticism") and those which are concerned to establish the best text when different readings are found to occur in different copies, which is the basis of textual (or "Lower", to use the 19th-century term) criticism — are as old as the bible itself, and so are attempts to find answers.

In this little book we shall venture only into the shallow end of a pool that is both broad and deep. We shall see that the critical study of the bible, that is to say, a careful, rational study, directed towards the solution of specified problems, has had a long history, whose beginnings are to be found, perhaps, already in the period when some of the books of the bible were still unwritten. We shall look at some of the earliest recorded attempts to explain how the bible came into existence and at some milestones in the development of the science, paying particular attention to the principles employed by biblical scholars through the centuries and to the reasoning which led them to their conclusions.

Notes

1   It ought to be said that, although we have used a Protestant bible as a specimen of this arrangement, the arrangement dates from a period long before there were any Protestants.

2   The Latin Vulgate has four books of Esdras (which is the Greek form of the name Ezra). I & II Esdras are those books otherwise known as Ezra and Nehemiah, respectively. III Esdras in the Vulgate is what the Greek bible calls I Esdras, a variant form of Ezra-Nehemiah, while IV Esdras, otherwise known as the "Apocalypse of Ezra", appears only in the Vulgate. With the first two almost universally known as Ezra and Nehemiah, III and IV Esdras have generally been re-numbered as I and II Esdras, but sometimes the double form of reference, I(III) and II(IV) Esdras, is employed to avoid confusion.

3   Notwithstanding its long use, especially in Ireland, as a personal name, in Hebrew *malachi* is a common noun, meaning "my messenger".

Chapter 2

Some Stages in the Development of the Critical Approach

(i)   Antiquity and the Middle Ages

When one begins to enquire about the origin and authorship of the books of the bible it may appear that a ready answer is available in the titles of the books themselves, at least in those cases where the title is also a personal name. It may easily be assumed that the books of Joshua, Samuel, Isaiah, Amos, Micah, and so on, were written by those bearers of the names whose activities or words are recorded in their respective books. Such an assumption is, perhaps, the more easily made in Christian circles inasmuch as the titles of almost all the books of the New Testament are clearly intended to indicate authorship, although the question of whether the authorship so indicated is accurate is one which we cannot pursue here.

It is not, of course, necessary to makc such an assumption, for nowhere in the books is it said that they were written by the men whose names they bear. In the case of prophetic books, the statement "these are the words of ..." may be seen as an attestation that the prophet *spoke* the words, but they do not imply that he wrote them down or compiled the book. (It may be worthwhile to notice, in passing, that in the case of two books no assumption of authorship has been made on the basis of their titles; no-one has ever suggested that the books of Ruth and Esther were written by those two ladies.)

However, even if we were to start with that assumption, we would be unable immediately to adduce authors for all the books. There are several which do not have personal names as their titles: Judges, Kings, Chronicles, Psalms, Proverbs, Ecclesiastes, Song of Songs, Lamentations. How may we identify the authors of these? In these cases one must probe beyond the titles; perhaps the book itself will convey some hint as to its authorship; perhaps a decision will have to be reached on other grounds. But even in the case of those books which have personal names as their titles it may not be safe to assume

7

that these are the names of the authors. The books of Samuel offer the clearest warning, for in a combined book of 55 chapters (31 in I Sam., 24 in II Sam.) the death of Samuel is recorded less than halfway through, in I Sam. 25. It can hardly be thought that he wrote the history of David's 40-year reign, to which II Samuel is devoted, which had not even begun at the time of his death. Clearly, on the basis of this example alone (the book of Joshua offers a similar though less dramatic example) it will be seen that the titles alone do not provide a sure basis for identifying authors. The quest for authors for the books bearing personal names as their titles must be pursued on the same basis as in the case of the books without them.

The considerations which we have here aired had already been taken into account by the men who in antiquity formulated answers to the question of the origin of the biblical books and whose opinions we may treat as amongst the earliest attempts to provide an answer to the question. In a *baraita* in the Babylonian Talmud, Baba Bathra 14b-15a[1], the question is posed, 'Who wrote the books of the bible?', and answered thus:

> "Moses wrote his book, and the portion of Balaam, and Job. Joshua wrote his book and eight verses which are in the Torah. Samuel wrote his book and Judges and Ruth. David wrote the book of Psalms by Adam, Melchizedek, Abraham, Moses, Heman, Yeduthun, Asaph, and the three sons of Korah. Jeremiah wrote his book, the book of Kings, and Lamentations. Hezekiah and his colleagues wrote Isaiah, Proverbs, the Song of Songs and Ecclesiastes. The Men of the Great Assembly[2] wrote Ezekiel, the Twelve, Daniel and the scroll of Esther. Ezra wrote his book and the genealogies of Chronicles up to his own time."

Some of these points were challenged in the course of the discussion which follows immediately after the passage quoted, but before we consider the objections we may note how far — at least in some cases — the early rabbis had moved beyond the "starting point" described above. Amongst the prophetic literature, where the presupposition of authorship by the person named in the title is easiest of all to make, only one volume, Jeremiah, is ascribed to the prophet himself.

No explanation is offered for this conclusion — nor for any of the other conclusions reached — but it may be supposed that the ascription of Jeremiah to the prophet himself is based on the statement in Jer. 36 that a book of Jeremiah's oracles was written — and re-written in an expanded form after its destruction — by Baruch at Jeremiah's dictation. The case of Jeremiah thus gives two insights into the workings of the ancient rabbinic mind. On the one

hand, it appears that the prophets were not automatically assumed to be the authors of the books bearing their names, and this appears, upon reflection, to be eminently reasonable. A prophet is the last person to be judged the author of a book of his oracles. Having spoken his word at the proper time his job was done; it would be for others to decide that the word was worthy of preservation. On the other hand, we see that where conclusions on questions of authorship might be drawn from statements made within biblical books this was done.

This latter principle clearly applied in the case of Psalms, Proverbs and the Pentateuch as well as Jeremiah. The names of David and those said to have been associated with him in the composition of the book of Psalms are either stated explicitly in psalm-headings or derived inductively from texts in individual psalms, while Prov. 25:1 has the heading "These, too, are proverbs of Solomon which the men of Hezekiah, king of Judah, copied". The word "too", in this verse, doubtless indicated to the ancient rabbis that Hezekiah's men had been responsible for collating or editing not only the other collections of Solomon's proverbs (which begin at Prov. 1:1 and 10:1) but also the two other books in the texts of which a connection with Solomon may be discerned (see Song of Songs 1:1, Ecclesiastes 1:1).

The reference in Proverbs to Hezekiah's men, along with the fact that certain biblical books contain clear indications of their composite nature (e.g. the sub-headings at Prov. 1:1; 10:1; 25:1; 30:1; 31:1), is the starting-point for the theory that various biblical books, including notably all the latter prophets with the exception of Jeremiah, reached the form in which we know them at the hands of editors. That Isaiah alone of all the latter prophets is assigned to Hezekiah's men rather than to the Men of the Great Assembly is an indication that the early rabbis had a historical perspective. Inasmuch as the preaching of the other pre-exilic prophets is included along with that of the latest prophets in the book of the Twelve the collection as a whole must be dated to the post-exilic period, hence its attribution to the Men of the Great Assembly, but the rabbis clearly did not perceive a need to assign Isaiah to a late date.   The attribution of Judges and Ruth to Samuel, of Kings and Lamentations to Jeremiah, of Ezekiel, Daniel and Esther to the Men of the Great Assembly, and of Chronicles to Ezra can all be explained on the basis of this historical perspective. That is to say, in all of these cases some significant figure, known from the Old Testament, can be held to have been nominated as author on no stronger grounds than that he lived at the end of the historical period with which the work in question is concerned. It may be that the authorship of the books of Joshua, Samuel and Ezra was decided on the basis of their titles, but

9

there may be another explanation for these attributions. All three men are credited with writing other books as well as those which bear their names and it may be that the attribution to them of their "own" books followed secondarily, after they had been, so to speak, first established as writers of biblical books in relation to those other books. In any event two of these attributions were questioned in the discussion which follows in the Talmud. It was pointed out that the deaths of Joshua and Samuel were recorded in their respective books, but this observation was countered by the suggestion that the book of Joshua was completed by Eleazar, son of Aaron, who added the account of Joshua's death and burial. This suggestion suffered from the weakness that the death of Eleazar is also recorded in Jos. 24, and so in turn the hypothesis was advanced that Phineas, son of Eleazar, rounded off the book with his notice of his father's death. The book of Samuel, in similar fashion, was deemed to have been completed, after Samuel's death, by Nathan the prophet and Gad the seer acting in turn[3]. The discussion was allowed to rest at this point without any acknowledgement that the nomination of supplementary authors in this way makes the assumption that Joshua or Samuel had any part in the writing of the books an unnecessary hypothesis.

So, finally, we come to the Mosaic literature. In the attribution to Moses of Job, as well as the pentateuch (with the exception of its last eight verses), and the reference to the inclusion of the portion about Balaam, there are three points of interest. The attribution of Job to Moses stems presumably from the presentation of Job as a patriarchal figure, but it is implicitly questioned in the talmudic discussion as to what period Job should be thought to have lived in. The suggestion that he lived in the period of the Persian empire, at least, would rule out the possibility of Moses having written about him. Secondly, the statement that Moses wrote the account of Balaam in Num. 22-24 appears to be an answer to an unrecorded question about the origin of these chapters: How could Moses, who was with the Israelites in the plain while Balaam pronounced his blessings on them from the heights above, have known the details of these contemporary events in which he had no part? The challenge to the idea of Mosaic authorship of this part of the pentateuch is turned aside by the assertion that Moses wrote it.

Thirdly, the suggestion that Joshua wrote the last eight verses of Deuteronomy is a concession to the argument that Moses would not have been able to record his own death. This point of view is later disputed and the suggestion made that Moses might very well have written of his death at divine dictation and, with the two possible verdicts stated, the matter was allowed to rest. The most interesting point of all that arises from this passage is that the Mosaic authorship of the pentateuch — which stems not from the title[4] but from the statement in Deut. 31:9 that "Moses wrote this Torah" — although it clearly was widely accepted, was already being questioned amongst Jewish scholars, at least with respect to two points, at the beginning of the Christian era, as it was to be questioned in all succeeding ages down to our own.

The question was raised, for example, by Abraham ibn Ezra in the twelfth century, albeit in a somewhat circumspect manner. Commenting on the phrase "beyond the Jordan" in the first verse of Deuteronomy — "These are the words which Moses spoke to all Israel beyond the Jordan" — he wrote

> If you understand the secret of the twelve, and of 'and Moses wrote', and of 'and the Canaanite was then in the land', and of 'in the mountain of the LORD it will be provided', and of 'behold, his bedstead was a bedstead of iron', you will discover the truth."

This cryptic comment indicates that the reader who understands the "secret" of the five other texts cited will understand the truth implicit in the text under consideration, which is that, as the place where Moses delivered his farewell address to the Israelites could only be described as "beyond the Jordan" by someone located on the western side of the river, where Moses never set foot, Moses could not have written it. Ibn Ezra made his point by drawing attention to several other passages in the pentateuch which, similarly, must be held to have been written by someone other than Moses.

"The twelve" probably refers to the last chapter of Deuteronomy, which has twelve verses, which records the death of Moses and praises him, saying that never since has there been a prophet like him; when this was written some considerable period of time had clearly elapsed since the death of Moses. Exod. 24:4, Num. 33:2 and Deut. 31:9 all say "and Moses wrote ...", and the natural inference is that somebody other than Moses wrote these words. The statement "the Canaanite was then in the land", which appears in Gen. 12:6, in the context of Abraham's travels in Canaan, can only have been written at a time when the Canaanites were no longer in the land, that is to say, after they had been ousted by the Israelites, and therefore after Moses' time. Again in connection with Abraham there is the statement of Gen. 22:14 "as it is said to this day, 'In the mountain of the LORD it will be provided'", which presupposes that at "this day", the time when the passage was written, Mount Moriah, the scene of Abraham's near-sacrifice of Isaac had been identified with the "mountain of the LORD", the site of the Jerusalem temple; and again a time long after the death of Moses is indicated as the point at which the statement originated. Finally, the notice in Deut. 3:11 that the "iron bedstead" (probably actually a sarcophagus) of Og, king of Bashan, was preserved, presumably in a kind of museum, at Rabbah, capital of the Ammonites, is not appropriate to the time of Moses.

Thus ibn Ezra offered half a dozen specimens of material in the pentateuch which cannot reasonably be said to have been written by Moses. The implication of this is that Moses did not write the pentateuch but ibn Ezra did not state this conclusion explicitly. Probably he found himself in something of a dilemma, torn between his respect for the traditional teaching of the rabbis, on the one hand, and his own observations, on the other, and it was not until a later period that the issue was pursued further.

(ii)   Early modern times

When the English philosopher Thomas Hobbes (1588-1679) published his work of political science *Leviathan* in 1651, he was concerned to establish the principles by which a state should be governed. Turning to the bible as a source of authority he was led, in turn, to enquire into the nature of the biblical books, their age and authorship. Starting from the principle that "the light that must guide us in this question [of who were the original writers of the books of the bible], must be that which is held out unto us from the Bookes themselves", he examined each book in turn.

The pentateuch, he concluded, was written not by Moses but "after his time, though how long after it be not so manifest". This conclusion was reached in three steps. First, he dismissed the argument from the title, which was familiar to him from the English Authorized Version, on the grounds that it no more follows that the "five books of Moses" must have been written by Moses than that the books of Joshua, Judges, Ruth and Kings must have been written by Joshua, the Judges, Ruth and the Kings respectively. Titles of this kind may denote either the authorship or the subject of a work. Next he pointed to the statement of Deut. 34:6, in connection with the death of Moses, that *"no man knoweth of his sepulcher to this day"*, and observed that, while it might be supposed that Moses could have written prophetically of his own death, it would have been nonsense for him to say that his grave was not known "to this day", that is, the time when the words were written and when Moses, if he were to be judged their author, was still alive. Thirdly, against the possible counter-argument that the last chapter of Deuteronomy might have been a post-Mosaic addition to an otherwise Mosaic pentateuch, Hobbes pointed to two other passages where a date of origin long after Moses is indicated: one is the note in Gen. 12:6, "the Canaanite was then in the land", which we have already encountered in ibn Ezra's commentary, and the other is Num. 21:14, where a quotation is cited from the Book of the Wars of the Lord. Since, as Hobbes said, this book recorded "the Acts of *Moses* at the Red Sea and at the brook of *Arnon*", and therefore must be dated after Moses' time, the work in which it is cited must stem from a time somewhat later still.

However, Hobbes did concede that Moses did write a book of law, which is referred to in Deut. 31:9, which he thought consisted probably of chapters 11 to 27 of Deuteronomy, and which he identified with the book which, according to II Kings 22:8; 23:1ff, was found, after it had been lost for a time, in the temple at Jerusalem in the time of King Josiah. This suggestion — at least that part of it which identifies Josiah's law-book with Deut. 11-27 — was to be fundamental to much scholarly work in later centuries.

The phrase "until this day", which clinched, for Hobbes, the post-Mosaic origin of the pentateuch, was used again as a touchstone in assigning the books of Joshua, Judges, Samuel, Kings and Chronicles, in all of which the phrase appears, to periods long after the events described in them. Ruth, likewise, may be assigned to a date after the events described in it on account of its reference in its opening verse to the time when the judges ruled, while in the case of Judges, where the phrase "*untill the day of the captivity of the land*" (18:30) indicates composition after the Assyrian conquest, and Kings and Chronicles, the contents of which carry the historical record down to the time of the Babylonian exile, Hobbes was able to point out explicit evidence of composition at dates long after events described in the books.

Ezra, Nehemiah and Esther, he thought, could have been written shortly after the events described in them, but he found no basis for dating Job, although he did observe that, while Job was "no fained person", the book is not history but philosophy. The Psalms, he suggested, were written mostly by David, but some were composed by Moses and "other holy men" (here Hobbes may be suspected of having broken the rule which he set down at the outset of his enquiry and relied on the titles of individual Psalms) but, as Ps. 137 reflects the experience of exile in Babylon and Ps. 126 reflects the return of the Jews, the collection cannot have been completed until the post-exilic period. Proverbs, too, is a composite work embracing sayings of Solomon (1:1; 10:1), Agur (30:1) and King Lemuel's mother (31:1), the finished volume being, in Hobbes' words, "the work of some other godly man that lived after them all".

Ecclesiastes and the Song of Songs Hobbes accepted as Solomonic, and most of the prophets he seems to have thought of as having written their own books. The exception here is the book of

Jonah, which is not prophecy (Jonah's only prophecy was "*Fourty dayes and* Ninivy *shall be destroyed*") but an uncomplimentary account of the man which he can hardly be thought to have written himself.

Having thus surveyed the Old Testament book by book, Hobbes finally concluded that the whole of the Old Testament "was set forth in the form we have it" after the return of the Jews from the Babylonian exile and before the time of Ptolemy Philadelphus when the Septuagint translation was made. He further suggested that the man responsible for the final shaping of the Old Testament was Ezra, and he cited as evidence II (IV) Esdras 14, in which Ezra, having bewailed the fact that "the law" had been burnt in the destruction of Jerusalem by the Babylonians, was enabled through divine inspiration to dictate in a period of 40 days to five writers working in relays a total of 94 books, 24 of which he was instructed to publish for all to read, while the other 70 were to be restricted in circulation to the wise.

We need not here concern ourselves with the question of the identification of the 70 esoteric books, or even with the question of whether or not exactly 70 possibilities may be nominated, but the 24 books intended to circulate freely are quite clearly the books of the Hebrew Bible and it may be surmised that this account, legendary though it may be, reflects the notion, which must therefore have been current in the first century of the Christian era (which is the date commonly assigned to II (IV) Esdras), that the "law" (i.e. the pentateuch), which is the primary concern of Ezra in the passage, dated not from the time of Moses but from the post-exilic age.

Another 17th-century philosopher who turned his attention to the question of the origin of the books of the bible was the Dutch Jew, Baruch (Latinised as Benedict, after he separated from Judaism) Spinoza (1634-77). In chapters 8, 9 and 10 of his *Tractatus Theologico-politicus*, published in 1670, he followed to some extent in the footsteps of Hobbes but at greater length and reaching some different conclusions, partly in consequence of his having the advantage, from his Jewish education, of access to Hebrew and Aramaic sources.

On the question of the authorship of the pentateuch he cited, with a full explanation, the passage from ibn Ezra's commentary on Deut. 1:1, which we have already examined, and added further points of his own to show that the pentateuch was written by someone who lived long after Moses. These further points were: 1) Moses is regularly spoken of in the third person and many of the things said about him, e.g. that he was the meekest of men (Num. 12:3), or that there never was a prophet in Israel like him (Deut. 34:10), must have been written by someone other than Moses; 2) the account of Moses' death and burial, especially in view of the statement in that context that "there never was a prophet like Moses" and that "no-one knows his place of burial to this day", clearly originated after Moses' time; 3) certain place names are used in the pentateuch although they were not current until long after Moses' time, particularly clear examples, being that of Dan, which appears in Gen. 14:14 (where Abraham is said to have pursued his enemies as far as Dan) although that place was not so named (perhaps it did not even exist) until the tribe of Dan migrated northwards, as described in Jud. 18:29, long after the death of Joshua; 4) events are mentioned in the pentateuch which did not occur until after Moses' death, e.g. the cessation of the manna is referred to in Exod. 16:35, although it did not occur until after the Israelites had crossed the Jordan (Jos. 5:12), or, again, Gen. 36:31 lists the kings who reigned in Edom before there was a king in Israel, and thereby acknowledges the existence of at least one king in Israel by the time the passage was written.

Similarly, Spinoza argued, the historical books from Joshua to Kings may be shown to have been compiled long after the events described in them. Further, he suggested that, since the books were clearly designed to follow one another consecutively, the whole corpus Genesis - Kings must have been compiled by one man. He nominated Ezra as the man who had set out to write, on the basis of earlier records — including the book of Moses which we find, albeit with additions by Ezra, in Deuteronomy — a "history of the Hebrew nation from the creation of the world to the entire destruction of the city (of Jerusalem)", but such matters as the duplication of material, with or without variation, and the chronological confusion which appears in various places in the pentateuch and former prophets, indicated to Spinoza that Ezra had not put the finishing touches to his work.

As for the other books of the Old Testament, Spinoza suggested that the Psalms were collected in the time of the second temple, and Proverbs at the same time or, at the earliest, in the time of King Josiah. The books of the prophets he regarded as anthologies and thus he was able to explain the chronological disarray of Jeremiah, the omission from the book of Jonah of Jonah's prophecies given in Israel and mentioned in II Kings 14:25, and so on. Daniel he dated, along with Ezra, Nehemiah and Esther, to the time of the Maccabees, although he considered chapters 7-12 of Daniel to have been written by Daniel himself. As for the origin of Job, he confessed himself undecided, although he inclined towards ibn Ezra's idea that it is a translation into Hebrew from some other language.

Sir Isaac Newton (1642-1727) does not normally figure prominently in the hall of honour for biblical scholars although he himself rated his *Observations upon the prophecies of Daniel and the Apocalypse of St John,* published posthumously in 1733, above his scientific works. The opening chapter of this work, entitled "Introduction concerning the compilers of the books of the Old Testament", is of particular interest as an exemplar of the principle of starting with what is found in the biblical text and thinking clearly through to whatever conclusions may follow. It is no less valuable if some of the conclusions reached are not entirely sound.

For his investigation into the authorship of the pentateuch, Newton first of all took the various references to the "book of the law" in the historical books to indicate the pentateuch and so he was able to conclude that King Jehoshaphat had it and used it as the basis for his reformation in the ninth century B.C. He also identified with the pentateuch the book found in the temple in the time of King Josiah (II Kings 22); therefore, he concluded, it must have been lost in the reign of Manasseh. So far his observations are not particularly significant — and his fundamental assumption that biblical references to the "book of the law" must necessarily indicate the pentateuch in the form in which we know it is probably questionable anyway — but he has indicated that "the law" existed in pre-exilic Judah.

From here he proceeded to locate the origin of the pentateuch in time by finding, first, the latest possible date and, next, the earliest possible date for its composition. For the first of these (the latest date) he observed that, since the pentateuch is accepted as scripture by Samaritans as well as Jews, it must have been compiled before the fall of the kingdom of Israel in 721 B.C. Newton was here associating the origin of the Samaritan sect with the account in II Kings 17 of how settlers, introduced to Israel by the Assyrians, combined their own religion with the religion of the Israelites, who had formerly occupied the land, in which they were instructed by a priest sent back from Assyria for the purpose. It may be noted, incidentally, that this picture of the origin of the Samaritans is probably quite wrong, but on Newton's thesis it follows that if that priest was able to instruct the newly settled deportees in "the law", "the law" (which Newton understood to be the pentateuch) was already in existence in Israel (the northern kingdom) before the exile.

Now, if the law was current in both Israel and Judah in the time of their independent existence then, since, being often in a state of enmity if not actually at war, neither would have borrowed it from the other, its origin must lie further back in history than the separation of the two states which occurred in the time of Rehoboam and Jeroboam. That is to say, the origin of the law must be traced back to the time of Solomon, at least, or even to David's time, if not earlier.

Newton happily took it back to the time of David on the grounds that in Ps. 78 David "quotes many historical things out of the books of Exodus and Numbers".

We may notice that two questions have been begged here: 1) that Ps. 78 was written by David, and 2) that references to incidents described in Exodus and Numbers could only have been learnt from those books and not from, say, earlier collections of similar material. However, we have followed Newton to his *terminus ad quem*, the latest date for the composition of the pentateuch.

His decision on the earliest possible date was reached quite simply on the basis of the list in Gen. 36:31-39 of the kings of Edom who ruled there before there were kings in Israel. From this Newton concluded, quite reasonably, that the passage could not have been written before Saul's time. He also concluded, though the basis for his conclusion is not clear, that this list of kings is carried down to the time of the writer. That is to say, he held that Edom was ruled by a king at the time the passage was written and so it must have been written before David conquered Edom.

If a book was known to David but not written before Saul's time a fairly short period is left to which its composition can be assigned (and the last point noted above narrows the limits even more), and so Newton decided that Samuel, once the burden of his office had passed to Saul, did the job of collecting and editing various writings of Moses, Joshua and, probably, others, into "the books of Moses and Joshua now extant". (He apparently saw no irony in saying that "the books of Moses and Joshua" were written by Samuel.)

On similar grounds of necessity in dating, Newton concluded that Samuel had written Judges and Ruth and the first part of Samuel, that is, up to the point at which his death is recorded, while the rest of the book was written by his disciples. Just about everything else in the Old Testament — certainly the historical books, Kings and Chronicles, the prophets and the psalms (some of which are patently exilic in origin) — he thought was written, or edited, by Ezra.

In this summary we have noted several instances in which questions have been begged or unwarranted assumptions have been made but for all that Newton is to be commended for having grasped firmly the important scientific principle of reasoning from observed data to whatever conclusion arises. It must also be acknowledged that this work was totally original, in the sense that it was his own and did not depend on earlier work by anybody else. The only reference made to any earlier opinion is his remark that "they judge well therefore who ascribe to Samuel the books of Joshua, Judges and Ruth", but who "they" might be is not at all clear. The present writer knows of no-one, apart from Newton, who has attributed Joshua to Samuel.

17

At another point in his work, Newton displayed his lack of familiarity with biblical scholarship when he referred to the Jewish division of the canon into Law, Prophets and Hagiographa, and defined the latter as Joshua, Judges, Ruth, Samuel, Kings, Chronicles, Ezra, Nehemiah, Esther, Job, Psalms, "the books of Solomon", and Lamentations. In other words, he presumed the Jewish conception of the prophetic literature to be the same as the Christian, and that the Writings, or Hagiograha, must be everything apart from this and the Law, but in this he was quite wrong (see Appendix 1).

(iii)   The beginnings of modern biblical criticism

A new impetus to biblical studies, which contrasts strongly with the work of Newton and his predecessors, came from a French professor of medicine, Jean Astruc, when in 1753 he published his *Conjectures of the reminiscences which Moses appears to have used in composing the book of Genesis.* While it may seem curious that he should have thought of Moses as the author of the pentateuch, a thesis which had been brought into question especially in the period immediately prior to Astruc's time, his suggestion that earlier sources are discernible in the book of Genesis was to become a milestone in the history of biblical scholarship. His suggestion was based on the observation that the two different ways or referring to God, viz., by the common noun "god" (in Hebrew, *elohim*) and by the proper noun "Yahweh", which is represented in English translations by "the LORD"[5], reflected the use by the compiler of Genesis of two different sources each of which had employed one of these distinctive forms of reference to God. Astruc envisaged Moses as having written the book of Genesis in four columns. For column A he utilized an "Elohist" source (i.e. one which employed the common noun *elohim* as its normal form of reference to God); for column B a "Jehovist" source (i.e. one which used the personal name Yahweh, or "Jehovah"); while in columns C and D he had inserted material derived from other minor sources. The idea of a compilation in columns which became confused in the process of copying during subsequent generations was perhaps somewhat simplistic, but the basic notion of "J" (for Yahwist or, in German orthography, Jahwist) and "E" (for Elohist) sources is still with us.

In the century after Astruc his basic point was further developed and a number of different proposals were made to account for the origin of the pentateuch. By the end of the eighteenth century the profesional biblical scholar was beginning to emerge and the first half of the nineteenth century saw the First Documentary Theory (as

18

proposed by Astruc and developed by Eichhorn) give way to the Fragmentary Hypothesis of Geddes (a Scottish Roman Catholic priest, who concluded that the pentateuch was compiled in the time of Solomon from numerous fragments which had originated from one or other of two circles which used one or other of the two forms of the divine name, Yahweh and *elohim*), and the Supplementary or Development Hypothesis of de Wette and Ewald (according to which the pentateuch is basically an "E", or Elohist, document which has been supplemented by other material). Ewald later abandoned this theory in favour of another which saw the pentateuch as an amalgamation of five or six separate works, combined in the reign of Jeroboam II by a "J" (Yahwistic) editor who also added much material of his own. This suggestion marked the beginning of the New (or, Second) Documentary Theory which received its final form at the hands of Graf and Wellhausen and which is still widely held at present.

This hypothesis envisages the pentateuch as the result of the amalgamation by stages of four basic documents (hence its alternative name, the Four Document Theory), although it also allows for the existence of other documents. There were a "J" (Yahwist) document, written around 850 B.C., and an "E" (Elohist) document, written around 750 B.C., both of which were combined to form a "JE" document around 650 B.C. A third document — "D" — consisting of the bulk of the book of Deuteronomy (hence the siglum) and identified with the book of the law found in the temple at Jerusalem in 621 B.C. (as described in II Kings 22), was considered to have been written shortly before that date and added to "JE" to form "JED" around 500 B.C. The fourth document, called "P" (for Priestly, because of its special interest in cultic matters) was held to have been written around 450 B.C. and added to "JED", providing a framework for the whole completed work, around 400 B.C., thus producing the pentateuch as we know it.

In the century which has elapsed since Wellhausen brought this theory to its classical form, a number of different approaches have been employed, some of them carrying "documentary" research further and some attacking the problem of the origin of the pentateuch from completely different viewpoints. The development in the early years of the twentieth century of the Form-critical method led to increased interest in small literary units which it seeks to classify according to their form and to evaluate against their original cultural setting. The Traditio-historical method is, as its name implies, concerned to study the history of traditions, that is to say, its concern is with the ways in which literature, which has been handed down over a long period of time (probably in oral form for much of this time) is shaped in the first place and modified in the process of its transmission. While these two methodologies have dominated Old Testament scholarship in recent years, a full study of them is, from our present point of view, quite definitely another story, but it may be mentioned that although they have abandoned the idea of documents as envisaged by earlier generations of scholars, the notion of "J", "E" or "P" material, or of writers or traditionist-circles labelled by the same sigla, is still very much alive in both schools of thought.[6]

Note on Moses and the Pentateuch

Much of our survey of the historical development of biblical criticism has been taken up in recording the reasons, advanced in various periods, why the pentateuch should not be considered to have been written by Moses. These arguments show that Mosaic authorship of the pentateuch is an accepted idea of long standing but we have not, in our survey, encountered any arguments in its support and so we may well ask why it should have arisen and survived.

It might be thought that the titles given to the books Genesis to Deuteronomy in the English bibles (especially the Authorized Version) — the First, Second, and so on, books of Moses — provide a starting-place for the theory of Mosaic authorship, but these titles have no long history. They are, in fact, the creation of the translators. They reflect the widely-accepted theory and cannot be used as evidence in its support. So, where, when and why did it start?

The source in Judaism (from where, it seems likely, Christianity derived it) for the traditional idea is the Talmud, where, although two opinions are offered as to who recorded Moses' death in the last chapter of Deuteronomy, there is unanimity on the question of the authorship of the rest of the pentateuch. But why, we may ask, did the ancient rabbis hold that Moses had written it, give or take the last several verses?

Already in the Old Testament itself, among fourteen references to the "law of Moses", there are four (Jos. 8:31; 23:6, II Kings 14:6, Neh. 8:1) references to the "book of the law of Moses" and four others (I Kings 2:3, Dan. 9:13, Ezra 3:2, II Chr. 23:18) which indicate that the "law of Moses" was something written. There are also four passages (Ezra 6:18, Neh. 13:1, II Chr. 25:4; 35:12) which mention "the book of Moses", and in one of these (II Chr. 25:4) the phrase stands in apposition to "the law", but precisely what body of written material is referred to in any of these passages is an open question. To be sure, by New Testament times the whole of the pentateuch was known as "the Torah" ("law"), "the law of Moses", or "the book of Moses" and so, ever since then, it has been easy to see these Old Testament passages as referring to the complete pentateuch, but there is nothing in any of the passages to compel the drawing of such a conclusion.

In a few places (e.g. Jos. 8:31, II Kings 14:6, Neh. 13:1, II Chr. 25:4) citations are given from, or reference made to passages in the book of Deuteronomy, but in others (e.g. Ezra 6:18, Neh. 8:14-15) things said to be written in "the book of Moses" or in "the law" do not appear at all in the pentateuch as we know it. It may well be that different collections of legal material are indicated in various passages, all of them attributed in their time to Moses but only some of which have found their way into the pentateuch.

Four times within the pentateuch it is recorded that Moses committed something to writing. He is said to have written "all the words of the LORD" (Ex. 24:4), the ten commandments on the stone tablets (Ex. 34:27f), a list of the Israelites' staging-posts in the desert (Num. 33:2) and "this Law" (Deut. 31:9). If there is a single point of origin for the theory of Moses' authorship of the pentateuch, it is probably this last verse, for to anyone to whom the word "torah" indicates the pentateuch, the statement "Moses wrote this torah" must say that he wrote the five books. Yet, as ibn Ezra observed eight centuries ago, the natural implication of the use of the third person is that someone other than Moses was responsible for writing these words. The more rational interpretation of all four verses is that someone, writing at some date after Moses' death, wished to testify to his belief that written records, both of legal and other material relating to the Mosaic age, had originated in that period, at the hand of the lawgiver himself.

There is an argument in support of Mosaic authorship of the pentateuch which is sometimes encountered in Christian circles and which runs like this: Jesus said the pentateuch was written by Moses and, since Jesus must have known the truth of the matter, his judgement must be accepted. Quite apart from the fact that the gap between the two halves of this statement is unbridgeable except by means of dogma, the argument rests on a series of assumptions: first, that Jesus actually said the words attributed to him in the gospels and they are not the free composition of the evangelists; second, that Jesus actually understood Moses personally to have written the pentateuch from Gen. 1:1 to Deut. 34:12; third, that Jesus intended his statements to stand as a permanent authoritative statement on the matter.

Even if the first assumption be granted — and that may be difficult in view of the fact that the crucial reference to Moses in the most important passage for this theory (Mark 12:26 and its parallel Luke 20:37) is missing from the parallel passage in Matthew — the possibility that Jesus, in using the terms "law of Moses" or "book of

Moses" or, simply, "Moses", as a means of reference to the pentateuch, was simply speaking in the language of his contemporaries cannot be discounted and offers a more realistic interpretation of the data. He could not, after all, have referred the Sadducees, in the passage mentioned above, to Exodus 3:6 by the modern method of citing chapter and verse.

Although the theory of Mosaic authorship of the pentateuch was widely held at the beginning of the Christian era it appears to have no firm basis. It breaks down, as we have already seen, on the presence within the pentateuch of passages which patently date from long after Moses' time and of complimentary remarks about Moses which he cannot be thought to have written himself. Once certain parts are denied to Moses, it is inevitable that the question be asked whether any of it can be attributed to him.

No-one has yet found any reason to think so, but to say this is by no means to deny the genius of Moses or to belittle his achievement. That the lawgiver, the mediator of God's covenant with Israel, the founder of Israel's distinctive religious tradition, stands ultimately behind the formation of that religion's fundamental textbook can hardly be denied, but that he was its author in the sense apparently implied by the headings in the Authorized Version can hardly be entertained.

Notes

1 The Talmud is an extensive compendium of rabbinic lore, presented in the form of discussion and commentary on the Mishnah (a codification of Jewish religious law published around 200 A.D.) which was produced in rabbinic academies in the period 200-500 A.D. There are two versions of the Talmud, the Babylonian and the Palestinian (commonly, though erroneously, called the Jerusalem Talmud). A *baraita* is material which derives from the *Tannaim* (the authorities whose teachings are preserved in the Mishnah and who lived before 200 A.D.) although not included in the Mishnah.

2 The Great Assembly was a legendary assembly of 120 elders, judges, prophets, sages, teachers and scribes who, according to rabbinic traditions, returned from the Exile with Ezra, drew up new rules, regulations and restrictions and laid the foundations of the Jewish liturgy.

3 This suggestion has its origin in I Chr. 29:29, which cites as a source of further information on David's reign "the books (or records or chronicles) of Samuel the seer, of Nathan the prophet, and of Gad the seer". The reference is, in all probability, to what we know as the books of Samuel, and so the rabbis understood this verse as a statement about the authorship of those books. If this really was the intention of the writer of Chronicles, we can push the date of the beginnings of critical enquiry into the authorship of scripture back at least as far as the time at which he wrote (probably around 400 B.C.). However, the verse is probably better translated:

Material about King David, from beginning to end, is written along with the material about Samuel the seer, and Nathan the prophet, and Gad the visionary",

and understood as referring not to authorship but to that work, or that section of a larger work (perhaps the Former Prophets, treated as a unit), in which Samuel appears at the beginning, Nathan in the middle (II Sam, 7,12) and Gad at the end (II Sam. 24).

4   The familiar titles found in many English bibles, "The First (Second, etc.,) Book of Moses, commonly called Genesis (Exodus, etc.,)" are of relatively recent origin. As we have seen already (see Appendix 1), the books of the pentateuch are known in Hebrew by their opening words and the titles in common use are (with the exception of Numbers, which is the only title translated) Latinised forms of Greek titles introduced by ancient Greek translators. The titles which involve the name of Moses were, similarly, the invention of post-Reformation translators and it is interesting to note that whereas recent printings of the Authorized Version give precedence, by the use of a larger typeface, to the titles "Genesis", "Exodus", and so on, this is a reversal of the practice of the first edition (1611), where the titles "First (Second, etc.,) Book of Moses" were given greater prominence. In Germany the titles I Moses, II Moses, etc., became standard usage.

5   The form "the LORD" (in capitals) is to be distinguished from the form "the Lord" in that the former represents the personal name "Yahweh" while the latter is the common noun which (without the capital L) is also used with reference to humans (and in modern Hebrew usage signifies "sir"). That the personal name was originally pronounced "Yahweh" is quite certain, although Jewish reticence about articulating the name (a very ancient practice which may be either based on or reflected in Lev. 24:16) led to the substitution in speech and scripture-reading of the word *adonay* ("my lord", whence the conventional translation), although the name "Yahweh" continued to stand in the text of the bible. Hebrew is normally written in a consonantal alphabet and, when vowel signs were added to the biblical text in the early middle ages, the vowels of the substitute word *adonay* were attached to the consonants of the proper noun Yahweh, following a convention which is described in the next chapter (see p. 33), thus giving rise to the hybrid form Yehowah or, in the form which became common, Jehovah.

6   For a detailed treatment of Old Testament scholarship in the last hundred years see R.E. Clements, *A Century of Old Testament Study* (1976). On Form Criticism and Traditio-historical Criticism see, respectively, G.M. Tucker, *Form Criticism of the Old Testament* (1971), and W.E. Rast, *Tradition History and the Old Testament* (1972).

Chapter 3

Some Basic Principles

(i)   Source Analysis

In the last chapter we saw that an important stage was reached in the development of the critical approach to biblical study with the observation that it is possible to detect, within biblical books, sources utilized by the authors of those books in their compilation. It is nowadays axiomatic that almost every book of the bible underwent a process of development, revision and editing, before it attained its final form. Yet it is worthwhile to reflect on some of the basic principles which have led to this conclusion, for no conclusion can be fully understood unless the reasoning by which that conclusion was reached is also fully understood.

It may be observed at the outset that the suggestion that traces of older sources may be discerned in the biblical writings is hardly strange in itself, since it is made clear in various places that the biblical writers did make use of earlier written sources. For example, in Num. 21:14 a piece of poetry is cited from a work called "the book of Yahweh's Wars", while quotations from another work, presumably an anthology of poetry, called the book of Yashar, or the Upright Man, appear in Jos. 10 and II Sam. 1, and throughout the books of Kings and Chronicles reference is made to various works which doubtless served as sources of material for the writers of those books.

Perhaps the most significant element in the rise of source analysis of the pentateuch was the Divine Name criterion which was first established by Jean Astruc. The suggestion that the variation in usage between the personal name Yahweh and the common noun *elohim* (god) might serve as a touchstone to differentiate between two originally independent sources appears to have been, in the first place, simply a piece of inspired guesswork on Astruc's part, but there is a firm basis on which to establish the principle, if not its detailed application. The evidence is to be found in Exod. 6:2, 3, which says:

God spoke to Moses and said to him, 'I am Yahweh. I appeared to Abraham, Isaac and Jacob as El Shaddai and I did not let them know my name Yahweh'."

Thus, it is said that Abraham, Isaac and Jacob worshipped Yahweh but did not know that name, yet as far back as Gen. 12:8 we read,

"Abram called on Yahweh's name."

In Gen. 15:2, we find,

"Abram said, 'Lord Yahweh, what will you give me ...',"

and so on. Notwithstanding the statement of Exodus 6:3, all three patriarchs are represented in Genesis as knowing and using the name Yahweh, and so it must follow that within the pentateuch there are two distinct and incompatible traditions about the origin of the use of the name Yahweh. The writer of Exod. 6:3, who held that this name was revealed for the first time to Moses, cannot have written those stories in which the patriarchs use the name, indeed, it may even be postulated that he could hardly have known them.

The Divine Name criterion, for all its importance in the development of the documentary theories, is actually one specific example of the more general principle, which applies not only to the pentateuch but to other biblical writings as well, that often phenomena may be discerned in a text which suggest that it has been compiled from two or more sources. It may be that inconsistencies are apparent, whether within a larger or smaller context (the Divine Name criterion is one example of inconsistency within a larger context; we shall shortly examine some cases of inconsistency in the smaller context), or it may be that two or more passages present what are essentially duplicate accounts of the same story which are unlikely to have originated from the same source.

The classic example of duplicate, or parallel, passages must be the first two chapters of Genesis. The two creation stories differ one from another, first of all, in their scope, chapter two concentrating on the creation of mankind, animals and vegetation, and making no mention of the sea, sky and cosmic bodies which feature prominently in chapter one. Thus far it might be possible to view chapter two as a detailed treatment of part of what is sketched in broad terms in chapter one, but this interpretation of the relationship between the two chapters is obstructed by their differences in order. According to chapter two, man was created before any vegetation existed, while the creation of all animals and birds intervened between the creation of the first man and that of the first woman, but in chapter one man and woman were created together on the sixth day, after the animals, while birds (as well as fish and other sea-creatures which have no mention in chapter two) were created one day earlier, and vegetation had already come into existence on the third day.

Alongside this, differences in language, style, and theology may be noted. God is called Yahweh in chapter two, but not in chapter one. In the first chapter he appears as a transcendent deity who brings about creation by his will, while in the second he appears almost in human form, moulding his creatures from clay as if he were a potter, planting a garden for his own pleasure, and proceeding by trial and error in the quest for a suitable mate for the man. Clearly these two chapters must have originated independently of one another.

To choose at random from the many possibilities available some further examples of duplicate or parallel narratives, it might be noticed that Jacob's name is changed to Israel in two separate places (Gen. 32:28 and 35:10). It is only after the second report of the change that the name Israel begins to be used, but even then its use is sporadic. This might suggest that the authors or collectors of some of the stories which relate to the latter part of Jacob's life did not know the tradition of the name-change. Or again, the birth of Isaac is announced twice, in two successive chapters (Gen. 17, 18) and causes as much surprize on the second occasion as on the first, the main differences between the two accounts being that in chapter 17 it is God who speaks to Abraham and in chapter 18 it is Yahweh, while it is Abraham who laughs at the news in chapter 17, Sarah in chapter 18. The two passages seem to be variations of the same story, the point being in the reference to laughter since the Hebrew form of Isaac is identical with the Hebrew word which means "he laughs".

Then there are the three stories in which a patriarch attempts, in dealing with a foreign ruler, to pass off his wife as his sister. In two of the stories the patriarch is Abraham (Gen. 12:10-20 and Gen. 20:1-18) and the foreign ruler is different (Pharaoh in Gen. 12, Abimelech, king of Gerar in Gen. 20) while two stories (Gen. 20 and Gen. 26:1-11) have the same foreign ruler (Abimelech) but a different patriarch (Abraham and Isaac, respectively). Because of the re-appearance of Abraham and Abimelech in more than one story, it is highly unlikely that three separate incidents are being recorded. It is much more probable that we have three versions of one story which have arisen independently.

As for cases where indications of diverse origin appear within a single narrative, one of the classic examples is the flood story of Gen. 6-9, in which various inconsistent details occur. For example, Noah is told to take into the ark one pair of each kind of animal, bird, and reptile (6:19f) and he does so (7:8-9 and again in 7:16) but between the command and its execution Noah is also told to take seven pairs of ritually clean animals and birds and one pair of ritually unclean kinds. Again, in one place (7:7-10) it is said that Noah and the livestock boarded the ark a week before the beginning of the flood, but in another (7:11-13) the embarkation is said to have happened on the very day that the rain started to fall. These and other details suggest that at least two different versions of the flood story have been combined to form the text as it now stands.

Another passage, one in which the hypothesis that two versions of a story have been combined offers a particularly neat solution to difficulties in a narrative, is Gen. 37, the story of Joseph's being sold into slavery. The section of particular interest begins at v.18, and two questions arise from the passage as it stands.

One question might arise from the fact that at two different points in the story two different brothers of Joseph dissuade the rest from killing him. In v.22 Reuben advocates leaving Joseph in the pit, while in v.27 Judah suggests selling him to some passing Ishmaelites. The question may not be a particularly cogent one inasmuch as Reuben's plan, as revealed to his brothers, would have meant killing Joseph, albeit by indirect means, but both brothers speak of not laying hands on Joseph. However, the major question arises from the section vv.25-28, in which both Ishmaelites and Midianites are mentioned, without the relationship between the two groups being made clear, and in which two verbs (in "they drew Joseph out of the pit" and "they sold him ... to the Ishmaelites") have no subject stated. If the subject of these verbs is to be understood as the Midianites, what may be supposed to have happened to the brothers' plan to sell Joseph? If the subject is the brothers, why would Reuben have expected to find Joseph still in the pit at vv.29,30, and what is the point of bringing the Midianites into the story at all? The question becomes even more prominent at the end of the story, for v.36 says,

"The Midianites sold him in Egypt to Potiphar ..."

although in v.28 Joseph had been sold (possibly by Midianites) to Ishmaelites, who brought him to Egypt, and in 39:1, where the story is taken up again after the diversion of chapter 38, it says,

"Joseph was taken down to Egypt and Potiphar ... bought him from the Ishmaelites who had brought him down there".

Clearly Joseph cannot have been transported to Egypt, and sold there, by two separate groups of people, so two different versions of

| Table 1(a) | : | **JOSEPH IS SOLD INTO SLAVERY, Version 1.** |

Gen. 37: 19 They said to one another, "Here comes this dreamer.

20 Come now, let us kill him and throw him into one of the pits. We shall say that a wild beast has devoured him, and we shall see what will become of his dreams".

21 Reuben heard this and delivered him out of their hands. "Let us not take his life", he said.

22 Reuben said to them, "Shed no blood. Throw him into this pit in the wilderness, but lay no hand on him". He said this in order to rescue him from their hand to return him to his father.

24 They took him and threw him into the pit. The pit was empty, there was no water in it.

25 Then they sat down to eat bread.

28 Midianite traders passed by and they drew Joseph up and lifted him out of the pit.

28 They took Joseph to Egypt.

29 Reuben returned to the pit and Joseph was not in the pit, so he rent his clothes

30 and returned to his brothers and said, "The boy is not there. "Where shall I go?"

36 The Midianites sold him in Egypt to Potiphar, an officer of Pharaoh, the captain of the guard.

| Table 1(b) | : | **JOSEPH IS SOLD INTO SLAVERY, Version 2.** |

Gen. 37: 18	They saw him from afar and before he came near to them they plotted to kill him.
23	When Joseph came to his brothers they stripped him of his robe, the long robe with sleeves that he wore.
25	They looked up and saw a caravan of Ishmaelites coming from Gilead, with their camels bearing gum, balm, and myrrh, on their way to carry it down to Egypt.
26	Judah said to his brothers, "What profit is it if we kill our brother and conceal his blood?
27	Come, let us sell him to the Ishmaelites, and let not our hand be upon him, for he is our brother and our flesh". His brothers listened to him.
28	They sold Joseph to the Ishmaelites for twenty shekels of silver.
31	They took Joseph's robe and killed a goat and dipped the robe in the blood.
32	They sent the long robe with sleeves and brought it to their father, and said, "We have found this. Do you recognise it as your son's robe or not?"
33	He recognised it and said, "It is my son's robe. A wild beast has devoured him. Joseph has been torn to pieces".
34	Jacob rent his garments, and put sackcloth upon his loins, and mourned for his son many days.
35	All his sons and all his daughters rose up to comfort him, but he refused to be comforted and said, "I shall go down to Sheol to my son, mourning". His father wept for him.
Gen. 39: 1	Joseph was taken down to Egypt, and Potiphar, an officer of Pharaoh, the captain of the guard, an Egyptian, bought him from the Ishmaelites who had brought him down there.

the story seem to be indicated. If we separate those parts of the story in which Judah and the Ishmaelites appear from those which mention Reuben and the Midianites, two parallel accounts of the incident, as set out in Table 1, result. In version 1, Reuben protects Joseph from his brothers by having him thrown into a pit, but Midianites steal Joseph and carry him off to Egypt. In version 2, there is no pit; the brothers are about to kill Joseph when Judah suggests selling him to some Ishmaelites, who are conveniently passing by, and they do so.

In this analysis only a part of the whole story — that part in which the problem of consistency appears — has been examined. It will be seen, however, that Joseph's splendid coat, the token of his father's special affection and therefore a cause for envy on the part of his brothers, is mentioned only in version 2, while Joseph's dreams, another cause for the brothers' disaffection, are referred to only in version 1. It is possible, therefore, that the section (vv. 5-11) which contains the account of Joseph's dreams, and that (vv. 3-4) which introduces the special robe, were originally separate and formed beginnings to version 1 and 2, respectively.

It is not easy to divide vv. 12-17 into two versions, but it is conceivable, from the fact that two places are named as the location of the brothers' sheep-pasturing (Joseph looks for them at Shechem, but finds them at Dothan), that originally one place was named in each version. If that is so, the two strands have been so cleverly interwoven that it is no longer possible to unravel them, and it is well to acknowledge such limitations to the enterprise of isolating sources.

It will be noted that in our analysis of Gen. 37, as in our examination of other places where reasons have been found for attributing different passages to different sources, no attempt has been made to identify any of these sources with the documents (J, E, D, P, etc.,) of classical source criticism. Our concern has been to explore the basic principles of this kind of study, to show that the postulation of diverse sources in the pentateuch is necessitated by the nature of the material. To follow this exploration through to its conclusion and to form a complete picture of the origin of the pentateuch, whether that be a documentary, a fragmentary or a supplementary hypothesis, would require vastly greater space than is at present available.

The main principles on which such an exploration should be based will, however, already be clear. Independent origins for individual passages may be postulated on the basis of inconsistency. Passages which agree belong together and passages which disagree stem from a different source from those with which they disagree. Once certain distinctions have been made, and two or more sources established, other passages may be found to agree with one or another of them on the basis of literary features or ideas.

In the category of literary features we may mention as potential indicators of different sources, in addition to the Divine Name criterion in Genesis, the use of two names for Jacob (he is sometimes called Jacob, even after his name was changed to Israel), or for the mountain of God (Sinai/Horeb), or the three names (Jethro, Reuel, Hobab) for Moses' father-in-law. To the realm of distinctive ideas belong the two different portrayals of God which we observed in Gen. 1 and 2, or the studious avoidance of anthropomorphic language when referring to the deity; in the narratives of Exodus and Numbers, Mount Sinai is sometimes seen as Yahweh's permanent residence, sometimes as a place to which he comes down in much the same way as Moses goes up to it; in the same narratives Moses acts sometimes on his own authority, sometimes in association with elders. All of these are potential indicators of diversity of origin for the material. So too, is the varied use of synonymous Hebrew words and expressions, the exploration of which is beyond our scope at present.[1]

(ii) Textual Criticism

As the primary interest of the study of any written document is in what its author intended to say, it is clearly important to be sure that the document accurately reflects its author's intention. With ancient documents, such as the books of the bible, there may sometimes be some doubt for one of two reasons. Our printed bibles, that is to say both our English (or other modern language) translations and our printed Hebrew bibles (and Greek New Testaments too, for that matter) are based on manuscripts of varying ages, ranging from the Dead Sea Scrolls, of perhaps the first or second centuries B.C., down to mediaeval manuscripts. There does not exist for a single book, or even part of a book, of the bible an original manuscript in the sense of the actual first copy as written by its author. So, when different manuscripts are found to contain differences in wording, questions arise as to which, if any, represents the author's wording and about how the variations occurred.

Secondly, even in places where there is no disagreement between different manuscripts, there may still be indications that the text no longer appears in the form which its author intended. A particularly clear example may be found in I Sam. 13:1, which says, "Saul was years old when he became king". Clearly, a number has dropped out from before the word "years", but what that number was is a matter for conjecture.

Textual criticism, as a method of establishing the original form of a text, has been developed and refined in the last century or so but the origin of this kind of study is very ancient indeed. Printed Hebrew bibles contain a system of marginal notes which have come down to us from rabbinic scholars in the early centuries of the Christian era or, perhaps, from an even earlier period — from the scribes of pre-Christian times — and many of these footnotes testify to the practice of textual criticism in antiquity. Because the text of the bible was sacrosanct in the eyes of the scribes and rabbis, even obvious errors which had occurred in the course of copying by hand, errors such as the mis-spelling of a word or the use of a singular verb where a plural one was needed, were preserved in the text itself and the necessary corrections noted in footnotes.

In order to draw attention to the correction, the uncorrected word, which continued to stand in the text, was supplied (after the invention of vowel-signs) with the vowels appropriate to the correction. It would usually be impossible to read the hybrid word thus produced and so the reader would be forced to turn to the footnote to find the consonants of the correction. This device is known as *kethibh* and *qere*, from the two Aramaic words used regularly in such footnotes: "X" is written (*kethibh*) but read (*qere*) "Y". A word which had accidentally been omitted from the text could be restored by means of a variation of this device, when a set of vowel-signs alone — meaningless without accompanying consonants — would direct attention to a footnote advising, "Read X (the consonants of the word to be inserted being here supplied), although it is not written", while the converse advice, "X is written, but do not read it" — which would apply most often when a word had erroneously been written twice — was signalled in the text by leaving unvocalized the word to be omitted.

If a simple corrective kind of textual criticism is thus attested, there is evidence also in rabbinic writings that the problem presented by differences between one manuscript and another was tackled long ago, usually by the simple expedient of following the readings found in a majority of manuscripts, an approach which may not always have led to the soundest conclusion but may in fact have created problems for textual critics in later ages. Some of the corrections advocated by means of the *kethibh* and *qere* device may have originated in study of this kind.

It may seem strange that the same scribes whose reverence for the biblical text prevented their correction of mistakes in it had no compunction about making deliberate alterations upon occasion, but they did so. They did this out of the same motives of respect and reverence for the text when they removed from it expressions which they considered offensive. The device *kethibh* and *qere* was some-times used as a means of substituting a euphemistic expression in the text. In addition, rabbinic literature has preserved a list of some eighteen places where the scribes are said to have altered the text of the bible in this way, but usually there is some indication in the text that something odd is afoot. Such action on the part of the scribes (known as *tiqqune soferim*, corrections of the scribes) is not, of course, textual criticism — it is, if anything, its antithesis — but the knowledge that this happened and the restoration of the Hebrew text to what it was prior to the scribal tampering falls within the sphere of the textual critic.

The type of simple correction mentioned earlier cannot easily be illustrated from translations because they have generally been adopted without comment by the translators, but the effect of the *tiqqune soferim* and their undoing may be seen clearly from a comparison of the English Authorized Version with more modern English versions. Thus, for example, when AV at I Sam. 3:13 says that God threatened to punish Eli's house "because his sons made themselves vile" (or "accursed", according to the alternative translation in the margin), its translators were doing their best with a Hebrew text which says, literally,

"because his sons were cursing to them".

The reason why the Hebrew text takes this very odd form is that, according to the rabbinic tradition, the text originally said

"because his sons were cursing God".

This was altered (the difference between "God" and "to them" is one letter in Hebrew) in order to remove such a distasteful statement from the text, but no doubt the scribes would have expected subsequent readers to understand its real significance. They would, after all, have as a visual aid the word "to them" which does not make sense in the context but looks like "God" which does. Modern translations, such as RSV, NEB, have followed the rabbinic tradition and restored the text to its original form.

Again, in Job 7:20, Job complains, according to AV,

"Why hast thou set me as a mark against thee, so that I am a burden to myself?"

but according to the list of *tiqqune soferim* he really said

"... a burden to you" (i.e. to God)

34

and the text was deliberately altered. Here, too, as in other cases, the modern translators have returned to the original text.

There is an important point to be made at this stage because the examples we have looked at (and there are many others) could be seen in another light. Approached solely from within the tradition of English bible translations it might appear that the modern translators are introducing changes in the biblical text as compared with the Authorized Version, which represents what is in the Hebrew bible. That is so, but it is important to note that these changes are not the result of recent study (much less of some possibly misguided policy of introducing change for change's sake) but they reflect the utilization of ancient knowledge of what the Hebrew bible originally said before it reached the form we know or what it would have said if those who handed the text down to us had been less circumspect about what they allowed it to say.

There are also places where the modern translations differ noticeably from the Authorized Version in consequence of more modern textual study, as may be illustrated by a comparison of the older and more recent versions and an exploration of the reason why changes have been made, but first of all, let us consider briefly some of the general principles of textual criticism.

Once it is established that there is a difficulty in a text, there are a few aids readily available to the textual critic. One is the existence within the bible of parallel texts, that is to say, a passage may be repeated in whole or in part elsewhere (e.g., parts of Kings re-appear in Isaiah; parts of various Psalms recur in other Psalms; Psalm 18 is identical with II Sam. 22) and a difficulty which occurs in one place may be resolved by reference to a "parallel" text. Another aid is the existence of the Ancient Versions, translations made in ancient times which may have been based on Hebrew texts slightly (or even, occasionally, substantially) different from the Hebrew text as it has come down to us. They may, therefore, attest the existence in antiquity of a different Hebrew text from that (or, those) which has survived. The most valuable Ancient Versions are the Greek translation known as the Septuagint, the Aramaic Targums, the Syriac version, and the Latin Vulgate. A third important tool is the recognition that errors in copying occur for certain reasons and that certain kinds of error recur. For example, words which look alike may be confused in copying by sight, while words which sound alike may be confused in writing from dictation. Rarely used words may be replaced by more familiar ones, particularly if either their sound or spelling is similar.

Quite often more than one such aid will be called upon in order to resolve a particular textual problem, as we shall see when we look at some examples of textual criticism at work. Naturally, it would be insufficient simply to find a different word in a parallel text or reflected in an ancient translation if there was no way of explaining why the change should have occurred.

Let us take as our first specimen of textual criticism at work Gen. 4:8, which is translated by AV thus:

> "And Cain talked with Abel his brother: and it came to pass, when they were in the field ..."

Clearly, there is something odd about this statement. What is the point of saying, "Cain talked with Abel his brother" when neither the content nor any consequence of the talking is mentioned? The Hebrew text says, literally,

> "And Cain said to Abel his brother",

using a verb which needs as its complement the words spoken. Manuscripts and older printed editions in Hebrew left a space at this point to indicate that some words were missing; AV's translators did their best to smooth over the difficulty by substituting the verb "talked", which may stand by itself. The Samaritan Pentateuch (not, strictly speaking, a translation, but another form of Hebrew text which stems from pre-Christian times) reads,

> "And Cain said to Abel his brother, 'Let us go out to the field'",

as do the ancient Greek and Syriac translations (which suggests that this phrase was included in the Hebrew text from which those translations were made) and all the modern English translations have restored the missing words.

In this case there is no obvious reason for the omission of the two words (let-us-go-out to-the-field), which have unaccountably dropped out of the Hebrew text, but a common reason for the omission of words is *homoeoteleuton*. This technical term is used to describe a situation where a copyist's eye has slipped from a word or phrase at one point in a text to the same, or a similar, word or phrase a little further on, with the consequence that he omits to copy everything which intervenes between those two occurrences of the word or phrase. This is what has happened in I Sam. 14:41.

In this passage the Israelite army is in trouble because Jonathan has had a taste of honey at a time when Saul had pronounced a curse against anyone who should eat before the end of the battle, and an investigation by means of the sacred lots is under way to find the cause of the trouble. The choice is to be made first of all between Saul and Jonathan, on the one hand, and the rest of the people, on the other. I Sam. 14:41 reads as follows, in AV:

"Therefore Saul said unto the LORD God of Israel, Give a perfect *lot*. And Saul and Jonathan were taken: but the people escaped".

Saul's request is not at first sight terribly meaningful, and the more one thinks about it the more obscure it becomes. Noting that the word "lot" is italicized (the device of the AV translators for indicating that a word had been supplied by them and is not represented in the Hebrew) we observe that what Saul said, according to the Hebrew text, was "Give perfect". The adjective in the Hebrew is, incidentally, plural, so the AV rendering, while representing a brave attempt to deal with a difficulty, can hardly be sound.

If we turn to the ancient Greek and Latin versions of this verse — which we may do conveniently by referring to the Revised Standard Version, in which the reading of these ancient versions has been adopted — we find that it is much longer, thus:

"Therefore Saul said, "O LORD God of Israel, *why hast thou not answered thy servant this day? If this guilt is in me or in Jonathan my son, O LORD God of Israel, give Urim; but if this guilt is in thy people Israel,* give Thummim. And Jonathan and Saul were taken, but the people escaped."

This clearly is the better text and the Hebrew text, as represented by our citation from AV, has suffered textual corruption in two ways. First, a copyist's eye has slipped from the first to the third occurrence of the word "Israel", with the result that the entire section emphasised in our citation from RSV was omitted, and, second, the word "Thummim", indicating one half of the sacred lot equipment, was misconstrued in the absence of its companion "Urim" and read as the adjective *thammim*, that is to say, "perfect".

An explanation is here called for of the Hebrew system of writing. The Hebrew alphabet consists of consonants only and the language was originally and is still normally written without vowel signs, but a system of vowel-signs, invented in order to assist with the reading of Hebrew at a time when the language was not in everyday use, was added to the biblical text around 600 A.D. Thus, any meaning which is dependent upon vowels reflects the opinion of those who inserted the vowel-signs at a relatively late stage in the bible's history and it is clear that sometimes the insertion of vowels (of "wrong" vowels, so to speak) caused words to be turned into something other than what was originally intended, as is the case in I Sam. 14:41, where *thummim* became *thammim*.

The nature of the Hebrew writing system means that occasionally two or more words with identical consonantal spellings may be equally satisfactory in a particular context and it will be impossible to decide that one is better than another. For example, the question of what exactly it was that Jacob leant on in Gen. 47:31 is an insoluble riddle. The Hebrew text of that verse says that he leant on the head of his bed (the word for bed being *mittah*), and so do the English translations. However, the writer of Heb. 11:21, quoting from the Septuagint translation which was made at a time before vowel signs had been invented, says it was the head of his staff (which in Hebrew is *matteh*). Thus, the translators of the Septuagint and those who supplied the vowel signs to the Hebrew text of Genesis had different opinions as to how the Hebrew word *mtth* should be read, but which of these would coincide with the opinion of the writer of Genesis it is impossible to say.

This is not, of course, a serious problem, and there are very few places where this kind of situation occurs, but the textual critic must be aware of the possibility that the misunderstanding of a word may have led to its being preserved in an erroneous form.

Amos 6:12 offers a nice example of how a wrong vocalization was introduced as a result of two words having been combined accidentally into one. If we approach that verse through its AV translation,

> "Shall horses run upon the rock? will *one* plow *there* with oxen? for ye have turned judgement into gall and the fruit of righteousness into hemlock",

we see immediately two italicized words, that is, two words supplied by the AV translators which are not in the Hebrew. To supply *"one"* as the subject of the verb "plow" is quite reasonable as a translation of the Hebrew verb which does not need a separate subject, but the word *"there"* is in a different category. Looking at this verse as a whole, the two questions in the first half must be understood as rhetorical questions which expect the answer "No". The verse as a whole is saying that, just as it is unthinkable that horses should run, or be allowed to run, on rocky ground, so it should be unthinkable that justice should be perverted into something poisonous, but this is just what the people have done. However, since the question "Does one plough with oxen?" would command the answer "Yes", the AV translators have attempted to reconcile it with its context by supplying the word "there". As in the other cases we have already

38

mentioned, they did their best according to their lights. However, if we go back to the Hebrew text we find the word translated "oxen" is not the usual one, *baqar*, a collective noun meaning "oxen", but as it were a plural form of this, *beqarim,* which is as erroneous in Hebrew as "oxens" would be in English.

The word *beqarim,* written in its consonantal form *bqrym* can be divided into two words, *bqr* (read *baqar* — oxen) and *ym* (read *yam* — sea). "Does one plough the sea with oxen?", a rhetorical question which expects the answer "No", suits the context, and this translation of the consonantal Hebrew text has been adopted in the newer translations, the textual difficulty which led the AV to supply an extra word having been explained as the result, first, of two words having been written as one and, second, of the perpetuation of this mistake by the addition of vowel signs to the erroneous compound word.

Finally we may mention as a source of textual corruption the confusion which can occur between Hebrew letters of similar shape and therefore of words containing these letters. While several letters display some similarity to other letters, the two letters most easily confused are *dalet* and *resh*, which have the phonetic values *d* and *r*, respectively. It is the confusion of these two letters which lies behind different versions of II Kings 16:6. AV reads,

> "At that time Rezin king of Syria recovered Elath to Syria, and drave the Jews from Elath: and the Syrians came to Elath, and dwelt there unto this day",

but the modern translations have "Edom" and "Edomites" instead of "Syria" and "Syrians".

The Hebrew name for Syria is Aram and the difference between this and Edom in Hebrew consonantal writing is only that one has *r* and the other *d* as its middle letter. The initial vowel is in both cases represented by the letter *aleph*, while the second vowel is, of course, not represented at all. Geographical considerations alone might lead one to the conclusion that Edom, the area to the south of the Dead Sea, would be more likely than Aram, the region around Damascus, to invade Elath (nowadays known as Eilat) at the head of the Red Sea, but a clue to the true intention of the biblical verse is to be found in Hebrew manuscripts. Some manuscripts, including the one used as the basis of modern scholarly editions of the Hebrew bible, actually say "Edomites", while others have a footnote of the kind mentioned earlier in this chapter indicating that although "Syrians" is written, "Edomites" should be read. The likelihood is, thus, that "Edom" should be read twice in place of "Aram" and the name Rezin, who was

39

king of Aram, not of Edom, should be deleted. Rezin, king of Syria, is mentioned in the previous verse and it is probably on account of this, coupled of course with the ease with which Edom could be misread as Aram, that the mistake occurred.[2]

Notes

[1]   For a fuller treatment of pentateuchal source criticism see N. Habel, *Literary Criticism of the Old Testament* (1971).

[2]   For a fuller treatment of textual criticism see J. Weingreen, *Introduction to the Critical Study of the text of the Hebrew Bible* (1982).

PART II

CRITICISM IN PRACTICE: THE CASE OF DANIEL

Chapter 4

The Starting Point

In this full-scale exercise in critical study of the Bible we shall investigate the book of Daniel. The questions which we shall explore, and to which we shall hope to find answers, are these: What kind of book is it? When (and, perhaps, by whom) was it written? For what purpose was it written?

Our aim will be, so far as it is possible, to find the answers to these questions in the book itself, for only there can we be certain that we are standing on firm ground. Our method of approach, therefore, will be to read the book, as though we were the first people ever to do so, to explore whatever issues may arise in the process, and to follow to their end whatever paths our enquiries may lead us along.

So we must begin by reading the book. But even before we can do that a choice has to be made, for the book of Daniel exists in two different forms. The difficulty does not lie in choosing one translation rather than another — any of the many English versions will suit our purpose, and it will probably be profitable to use more than one of them — but in deciding which of two books we are going to investigate. In Jewish and Protestant editions of the bible the book of Daniel has 12 chapters; in Catholic editions it has 14 and, in addition, chapter 3 is considerably longer than it is in other editions.

This situation may be explained up to a point from the history of the canon of scripture. In the Hebrew bible[1] Daniel appears in its shorter form; in the oldest Christian bibles, in which a Greek translation of the Old Testament is utilized, the longer form is found. It is commonly supposed that the Greek version of the Jewish bible which the Christian church adopted as its Old Testament was one which reflected a canon of scripture formulated in Egypt, where the Greek translation was made and used by the Jewish community, which differed in various respects from that which is customarily held to have been confirmed by Palestinian rabbis at Yavneh in the latter part of the first century of the Christian era. The Protestant reformers adopted the Hebrew canon as their standard, relegating the extra chapters of Daniel, as well as several other works, to the Apocrypha,

43

while the Roman church maintained its tradition of using the longer version, labelling the parts which Protestants call "apocryphal" "deuterocanonical", a term first employed by Jerome in the fourth century.

Thus, we may explain up to a point the fact of the two forms of Daniel. We have not, however, even approached the question of why these two forms should have arisen in the first place. It is surely legitimate to ask this question in the course of our investigation into Daniel, but it is scarcely appropriate to explore it at this stage, before we have examined the contents of the book. However, if we are to pursue the question we must obviously define the book of Daniel, for the purpose of our study, as including the apocryphal/deutero-canonical sections.

Another observation may be made at this stage, since it arises from the place which Daniel occupies within the Old Testament. In Christian editions of the bible Daniel is placed firmly amidst the prophetic books: sandwiched between Ezekiel and Hosea, it precedes the collection of small books known as the "twelve" or "minor" prophets and stands as the fourth of the four "major" prophets. In Jewish editions, on the other hand, Daniel does not appear amongst the prophets at all, but in the third section of the bible, the writings. Thus it would appear that two very different assessments of the book of Daniel were made in ancient times by those who assembled and classified the biblical library. A decision as to whether one of the assessments implied by the two positions of the book is to be preferred to the other will depend on the assessment of the book which we shall make for ourselves in the course of our study.

Let us turn, then, to examine the contents of the book with an eye to picking up any clues that may assist us in our investigation. Various points will be noted in the summary which follows.

Chapter one introduces Daniel and his three friends, Hananiah, Mishael and Azariah. All of them are members of the Jewish nobility, captured by Nebuchadnezzar in the third year of Jehoiakim and taken to Babylon where they undergo a period of training for three years in preparation for service at the royal court. They refuse the food and drink provided for them but live on vegetables and water, and are all the better for it. At the end of their training period they are found to be ten times better in insight and judgement than all the magicians and exorcists of the kingdom. A final note informs us that Daniel was there until the first year of Cyrus but we are given no such information about the others.

According to chapter two, Nebuchadnezzar, in his second year, had a dream which troubled him. He demanded that his wise men, magicians, and so forth, should tell him both what the dream was and what it meant. Since they were unable to satisfy even the first of these requirements, the whole lot — including Daniel and his friends — were to be put to death, but Daniel, through divine intervention, was able to tell the king what the dream was and what it portended. It predicted the course of history after Nebuchadnezzar's time. Daniel was rewarded by being given a high office ("regent over the whole province of Babylon and chief prefect over all the wise men"). He got good jobs for his friends, too.

Daniel does not appear in chapter three, in which his three friends refuse to conform with a decree of Nebuchadnezzar and worship the golden image which he had set up. They are thrown into a furnace but emerge unscathed and are further promoted in the imperial service. In the Greek and Latin versions and modern translations which follow the tradition established by these, chapter three is rather longer than it is in its Aramaic form. Between, as it were, verses 23 and 24 of the latter, the former versions have a long insertion[2], which consists of three sections. The first, known as the Prayer of Azariah (22 verses long), is followed by a short prose interlude which returns to the theme of the story. The fire is stoked up and an angel comes to join Azariah and his friends who then sing the long hymn (41 verses) known as the Song of the Three Young Men or, from its opening words in Latin, *Benedicite Omnia Opera*.

In chapter four Nebuchadnezzar recounts, in the first person, his vision of a tree chopped down, by order of a Holy One speaking from heaven, and left tethered in the grass for a period of "seven times", and how this was interpreted by Daniel as predicting the king's temporary loss of sovereignty and his banishment from human society to eat grass like an ox. Starting at verse 28 half a dozen verses record in the third person that this happened and then Nebuchadnezzar again takes up the story in the first person and recounts how he returned to his senses and his sovereignty. In conclusion he praises "the King of Heaven".

During a banquet given by King Belshazzar in chapter five, a hand appears and writes mysterious words on the wall. No-one can read the writing or say what it means. The queen reminds Belshazzar that Daniel, who was chief magician in the time of Belshazzar's father Nebuchadnezzar, is still around. He is brought in, reads the writing and declares that it announces the end of Belshazzar's kingdom. He is richly rewarded, and just in time. The prediction is fulfilled on that very night and Darius the Mede takes over.

In the reign of Darius, according to chapter six, Daniel, being one of three chief ministers, arouses the envy of his colleagues and subordinates who plot to do away with him. They contrive to have him thrown into a lion pit but when he is found still alive the next day he is brought out and his accusers are fed to the lions. Darius decrees that all his subjects should respect Daniel's god, and finally, it is said that Daniel prospered in the reigns of Darius and Cyrus.

The first verse of chapter seven introduces, and dates to the first year of Belshazzar, the vision which, beginning at verse two, Daniel describes in the first person, and which, according to Daniel's account, was explained to him by a bystander in the vision as symbolizing future history. From here on to chapter twelve, with the exception of a brief notice in 10:1, the book is written in the first person singular.

Chapter eight contains a second vision of future history. This one is dated in the third year of Belshazzar.

In chapter nine Daniel, pondering in the first year of Darius on Jeremiah's prediction of seventy years' ruin for Jerusalem, is told by "the man Gabriel" (who first appears in chapter eight) that "seventy years" means "seventy weeks of years". Daniel is told of various future events which are related to this time-scale.

Yet another vision of the future, this time dated in the third year of Cyrus, is described in chapters ten to twelve. An outline of events from the period of the Persian empire to "the end" is presented with considerable detail. Daniel is instructed to keep the vision secret until "the end".

Chapter thirteen is the story of Susanna, which is set in a Jewish community in Babylon. Two rascally elders attempt to seduce Susanna and, when she refuses to give in to them, denounce her as an adulteress. She is about to be convicted in court when Daniel, who is described as a young man, secures her acquittal through cunning cross-examination of the two elders who have given evidence against her. The incident is not dated.

Chapter fourteen, otherwise known as Bel and the Dragon, contains two stories set in Babylon in the time of Cyrus. Daniel appears in them as a King's Friend. In the first story Daniel demonstrates that the god Bel is only an idol. Cyrus thinks he must be a god because he eats vast quantities of food but Daniel spreads ashes on the floor of the temple just before it is sealed up for the night. In the morning the footprints of the priests and their families are clearly seen. In the second story the King points out that a huge snake (the dragon of the title) worshipped by the Babylonians cannot be put in the same category as the idol Bel, since it is obviously alive. Daniel feeds it cakes made with pitch, fat and hair until it bursts and thereby shows it not to be a god. Daniel is put in the lion pit for a week with seven hungry lions but is sustained with a bowl of stew brought to him by the prophet Habakkuk, transported by his hair and an angel from Judah for the purpose.

Notes

1   It should be noted, incidentally, that there is actually no Hebrew version of Daniel; approximately half of the book (2:4 - 7:28) is written in Aramaic.

2   It is not intended, by the use of this term, to prejudge the question of whether the passage was "inserted" in the Greek version or "omitted" from the Aramaic text.

Chapter 5

Preliminary Observations and their Implications

In summarizing the contents of the book of Daniel we have provided the most elementary kind of answer to the question of what the book is. In the process we have noticed various details, mostly to do with chronological matters, which invite closer scrutiny and which may be conveniently divided into two groups: those which relate to the life of Daniel and those which relate to the structure of the book.

The data which belong to the first group will be highlighted if we set out to construct, on the basis of the information given in the book, a biography of its hero. From the early chapters we learn that Daniel, taken to Babylon as a young man, reached a very high position in the service of Nebuchadnezzar. But already in these early chapters we may have encountered a problem. According to 1:5, he was to undergo a period of training lasting three years before entering the king's service and, as we are told in v.18f, he and his friends duly entered the king's service. It follows that chapter one covers a period of three years and, although the events of that chapter are not dated in terms of Nebuchadnezzar's reign, we must have reached by the end of the chapter at least the fourth year of his reign.[1] Yet, in the incident recorded in chapter two, which is dated the second year of Nebuchadnezzar, Daniel is already reckoned among the wise men of Babylon (2:13,18) and in consequence of the service he performs for Nebuchadnezzar in explaining the king's dream he is made "regent over the whole province ... and chief prefect over the wise men". If all this happened in Nebuchadnezzar's second year, which is to say, at the very least one year before Daniel's introduction to the court, we would indeed appear to have encountered a problem. Furthermore there is one detail in the story of chapter two which may complicate the problem, for although Daniel is already numbered amongst the wise men and is threatened with death on that account vv. 13,18) he is introduced to the king in v.25 as an apparently previously unknown Jewish exile, despite the fact that he has had a personal interview with

49

the king in v.16, presumably on the basis of his standing as one of the king's wise men. We should perhaps also note in this context that the picture presented in chapter thirteen of Daniel as a young man living apparently as a private citizen in a Jewish community is difficult to reconcile with the information in chapter one that from the time of his capture Daniel was domiciled in court circles.

Clearly the early stages of Daniel's personal history are attended by obscurities. We shall explore the implications of our observations in due course but for the present let us continue with our survey of the biographical material available to us.

Despite his rise to high office under Nebuchadnezzar, Daniel presumably lived as a private citizen throughout the reign of Belshazzar for, in 5:10ff, the queen finds it necessary to inform the king of Daniel's existence and reputation. We may well ask whether this retirement can be accounted for.

On Belshazzar's last night Daniel was elevated to the rank of "third in the kingdom" and he continued in a similar position under Darius, being one of three presidents superior to the satraps. According to 6:29 (verse 28 in the English versions), he prospered during the reigns of Darius and Cyrus, presumably keeping this job. Now, back in 1:21 we read "Daniel was there (in Babylon) till the first year of King Cyrus", which implies that he was no longer there after that time, either because he died or went elsewhere. The statement of 6:29 that he prospered during the reign of Cyrus may, though it need not necessarily, be taken to indicate that he was still in Babylon for more than one year of Cyrus's reign, but 10:1, which dates Daniel's last vision to the third year of Cyrus, sees Daniel still in Babylonia at that time, while 12:13 implies that Daniel's death followed shortly after this last vision. The question clearly arises, why should 1:21 say Daniel was there till the first year of Cyrus if he was still there two years after that?

If we turn now to examine the structure of the book two points will be immediately apparent: First, that it falls naturally into three parts — chapters 1-6, containing stories about Daniel and his friends, written in the third person; chapters 7-12, containing reports of visions experienced by Daniel and recorded in the first person; chapters 13-14, further stories about Daniel, again written in the third person. It is right that the stories of the first and third sections should be distinguished, for the two groups of stories display differences in their characterization of their hero and in their theological intent. In chapters 1-6 Daniel is a pious Jew who serves simply as a medium of divine revelation; although he is repeatedly commended by the various rulers for his wisdom and insight the reader must recognize that it is not for his own abilities that he receives preferment. The

Daniel of chapters 13 and 14, on the other hand, is a cunning fellow who scores over his rivals by the exercise of his native wits. Again, while the stories of chapters 1-6 convey the positive message of the superiority of Daniel's god over the gods of the Babylonians, those of chapter 14 have only the negative value of poking fun at idols and their worshippers.

The second point which emerges from an examination of the structure of the book is that while a chronological sequence is discernible in the overall arrangement of the book, in that it begins with the reign of Nebuchadnezzar and ends with that of Cyrus, with Belshazzar and Darius falling in between, a strict chronological order is not maintained throughout. Chapters 7 and 8, which are dated, respectively, in the first and third years of Belshazzar, belong chronologically before chapter 5, which deals with the end of Belshazzar's reign, while chapter 13, in which Daniel appears as a young man, obviously belongs, although no date is mentioned in it, to an early stage in his story. (The Greek version of Theodotion places this chapter at the beginning of the book.) Arranged strictly according to chronology the order of chapters would be as in Table 2.

It will be noted from this that, while the chronological order of the book as a whole is in some disarray, in each section of the book (i.e. in chapters 1-6; 7-12; 13-14) the chronological sequence is satisfactory. So it seems clearly to follow that the book has been deliberately arranged in these sections. The stories of chapters 1-6, the visions of chapters 7-12, and the appended stories of chapters 13-14 have been assembled in groups at the expense of the chronological coherence of the whole. It might even be suggested that there is here a strong argument in favour of concluding that the book of Daniel is actually three separate works laid end to end. While each section has its own chronology, there is an obvious cleavage between chapters 6 and 7 (and similarly between chapters 12 and 13), the material of the visions being different from that of the stories, and, as we have already observed, the two groups of stories (chapters 1-6 and 13-14) are to be separated from one another not only on the general grounds of their different outlooks but on the specific basis of the irreconcilable conflict which exists between chapters 1 and 13.

This leads us back to the area of the problems encountered in attempting to write Daniel's biography. Of the various questions raised above the easiest to resolve is that concerning Daniel's apparent retirement from public life during the reign of Belshazzar. Even without any reference to the chronology of the period it will be obvious that between the early years of Nebuchadnezzar and those of Cyrus some considerable period elapsed and that the book of Daniel cannot have been intended to present an exhaustive account of the

Table 2: The Book of Daniel, arranged in chronological order

Sequence of Chapters	Ruler	Year	Comments
1. 2. 3. 4.	Nebuchadnezzar " " "	Unspecified 2 Unspecified	Chapter 1 must precede chapter 2; chapters 3 and 4 must follow it.
13.	Unspecified		This chapter is the most difficult to place. Daniel is a young man, but already in Babylon, so it belongs after chapter 1, but there is no good reason to break into the sequence of chapters 1-4, in all of which Nebuchadnezzar plays a part.
7. 8. 5.	Belshazzar " "	1 3 last	This sequence is certain.
9. 6.	Darius "	1 Unspecified	The reverse order is also possible.
14. 10-12.	Cyrus "	Unspecified 3	Chapters 10-12 form a unit; if Daniel's imminent death is implied in 12:13, chapter 14 would have to come first.

career of its hero throughout the whole of this period. The book clearly reports only a handful of incidents from a long career. If, in the course of reporting on one such incident, it is implied that Daniel was for a time not active in public administration but no further information is given, there is no more to be said.

The case of the discord between 1:21 and 10:1 is rather different, for here we have two statements at variance with one another. It might be suggested that the two statements may be harmonized by the assumption that in the former verse the reference is to the duration of Daniel's official service and that when he experienced his last vision he was living in retirement. However, such an assumption is without warrant in the text and would, moreover, only solve the problem at the cost of creating another. If 1:21 is understood to mean that Daniel remained in the service of successive rulers from the early years of Nebuchadnezzar to the first year of Cyrus a conflict is created between this and 5:10ff, in which it is clearly implied that Daniel did not serve in Belshazzar's administration until that monarch's last night. It would be much safer simply to accept that discord exists between 1:21 and 10:1 and to explain it, recalling our observations on the structure of the book, as resulting from the conflation of formerly independent documents. The "story-book" of chapters 1-6 knew that Daniel's life in Babylon extended from the early years of Nebuchadnezzar's reign until the first year of Cyrus; the "vision-book" of chapters 7-12 knew that he was still alive and in Babylon in Cyrus's third year.

So we return to the problems which attend the beginnings of Daniel's story. As we have already seen, the conflict between chapter 13, in which Daniel appears as a young man living in a Jewish community in Babylon, and chapter 1, according to which Daniel was taken straight from Judah to the court of Nebuchadnezzar, can only be resolved by assigning to the two stories independent origins. This can be done the more readily in that the sections of the book in which the two stories appear may be declared on other grounds to have originated separately.

What of the conflict which was found to exist between chapters one and two? Can it be allowed that Daniel was not only already numbered among Nebuchadnezzar's wise men but promoted to be their chief before the completion of his apprenticeship and his admission to the court? There are two possible ways of resolving this conflict. On the one hand, it may be possible to alter the date in chapter two to something other than the second year of Nebuchadnezzar. On the other hand, it may be supposed that originally the stories in the first two chapters of Daniel were quite independent of one another.

The former possibility suffers from the weakness that there is no textual-critical basis for the change; its adoption would be simply a cavalier change made in the interests of convenience. The latter possibility is the more satisfactory in that it recognizes that the conflict arises only out of the juxtaposition of the two stories. It may, further, be supported, albeit in an indirect way, by the other curious detail of chapter two which we noted above. Although Daniel is already numbered amongst the wise men and is threatened with death on that account he is introduced to the king in v.25 as an apparently previously unknown Jewish exile. So there is an inconsistency within chapter two as well as between it and chapter one and the most reasonable explanation for this is likely to be that the story of chapter two has been modified in the course of its own history. If a story, in which an unknown Jewish exile called Daniel was first introduced to King Nebuchadnezzar because he was able to solve a problem which had foxed all the king's professional advisers, was to be attached to another story, in which Daniel was already based in Nebuchadnezzar's court, some modification of the former story would be necessitated in order to avoid an obvious conflict. On the basis of our observations we may conclude that this is what has happened in the case of Daniel chapter two; we must also recognize that whoever introduced the modification made a less than perfect job of it, leaving behind, in v.1 and v.25, two clues to the original state of affairs.

To summarize our findings so far, on the basis of our observations on the structure of the book and on the chronological data provided in it it may be concluded that the book of Daniel as we know it has been compiled from various elements, which existed independently before they were brought together. We have found reason to think that the three sections of the book may once have existed independently of one another, while within the first section at least, there is evidence that its constituent stories (or two of them, at any rate) existed separately before being combined.

Another question which may be asked at the present stage of our enquiry is, when was the book written (or compiled)? Outside limits may be readily adduced, for the book cannot have been written before the incidents recorded in it took place. Thus the third year of Cyrus's reign — the date of Daniel's last vision — must be the earliest possible date for the completion of the book; although individual parts (chapters) of it could have been written earlier, no part can be earlier than the beginning of the reign of Nebuchadnezzar. The latest possible date has to be fixed on the basis of external evidence. We can say that the book was in circulation by the beginning of the Christian era because copies of it have been found at Qumran and it is cited in the New Testament. Between the outer limits thus established there lies an interval of some four or five centuries. Can we not date the composition of Daniel with greater precision than this?

Perhaps the logical place to begin is with Daniel himself. Can it be suggested that he had, or could have had, a hand in the making of the book, or even that he wrote it himself? If the conclusions which we have already reached are valid, if the book contains different and mutually exclusive accounts of Daniel's emergence to prominence, it is clear that it could not all have been written by Daniel and that he cannot have been its compiler either, but is it possible that he might have written some of it?

The obvious implication of the use of the first person singular throughout chapters 7-12 is that Daniel himself wrote these chapters. In addition, it is implied at two places in the book that Daniel wrote *something* down. These places are 8:26 and 12:4,9. In 8:26 Gabriel advises Daniel, after giving him an explanation of the vision in that chapter, that "you must keep the vision secret", while similar advice is given in chapter 12:

"Keep the words secret and seal the book till the time of the end" (12:4) and
"the words are kept secret and sealed till the time of the end" (12:9).

In these passages, certainly in 12:4, it is implied that Daniel wrote an account of his visions — or, at least, of the vision of chapters 10-12 (and perhaps also of that in chapter 8) — for if Daniel was to seal the book he must surely have written it first.

May it be inferred that the book referred to in 12:4 is the book of Daniel? Might it be rather chapters 10—12 only? A possible argument in favour of the latter possibility, or at least against the former one, may be found in the first verse of chapter 10, where a statment in the third person, to the effect that Daniel had a vision, had difficulty in understanding it but eventually managed to do so, precedes the account of the vision, given in the first person, which begins in verse 2. Chapter 7, which contains the account of Daniel's first vision, begins in similar fashion, with a report in the third person that Daniel had a dream which he recorded in writing, and "here his account begins".

The latter passage suggests clearly that someone other than Daniel has provided a framework for an account written by Daniel, and the former passage has the same function. So, in answer to the question whether Daniel might have had a hand in the writing of the book, we may say that the book clearly suggests that Daniel wrote accounts of his visions which have been incorporated, along with other material, by an editor in the book with which we are familiar. The hand of the editor may be seen not only in the introductions to Daniel's visions but also, as we have already suggested in chapter 2, and in chapter 4, where he contributed the third-person passages to what we must, if we are to hold chapters 7-12 to be from the hand of Daniel, declare to have been written by Nebuchadnezzar himself.

Of course, we may well ask whether we should accept the statements, explicit or implied, of the book about its origins at their face value, but to be able to answer the question we shall have to engage in further study of the book. Since the book is basically historical we may subject it to historical criticism. If we compare the historical information contained in Daniel with what we know of Babylonian and Persian history from contemporary records and classical sources we may well be able to draw some conclusions as to whether Daniel was written in the period with which the book deals. We shall, in any event, have to undertake this exercise in order to assign a date to those parts of the book for which no author has yet been nominated and, indeed, in order to be able to decide at what period in history the editor (hypothesized) should be located. But before we turn to this task we must note one further conclusion which may be drawn from the observations which we have already made.

Quite apart from what the book of Daniel may be thought to indicate about its authorship, it does give a pretty clear indication of the date of its publication. It does this in 12:4, 9, where Daniel is bidden to "seal the book till the time of the end". If the reference here is to the whole book of Daniel (and notwithstanding the conclusions we have reached above, it may have been the intention of the writer that it be so understood), then we can date the publication of the book to the time which is considered in the book to be the "time of the end". If the reference is to only a part of the book — say, to the collection of visions, or even to chapters 10-12 alone — then we can date the publication of that part, at least, and, if that has been incorporated into the larger work by another party, the date of publication of the longer work will be somewhat later.

The date of the "time of the end" will have to be ascertained by a study of those sections of the book in which the future is revealed to Daniel. Thus, we have set ourselves two tasks which we shall pursue in the following chapters.

Notes

1   A detailed study of the chronology of the period would be out of place here, but will be undertaken below. See pp 58f.

Chapter 6

Daniel's Life and Times

As we embark on our study of the historical data of the book of Daniel which relate to the period in which Daniel is represented as living, we must consider what expectations we may hold for the outcome of the study. Obviously, if the book was written in whole or in part by Daniel himself, or by a contemporary of his, we might expect that it would display an accurate knowledge of the history of the time. (It might even be an important source of knowledge for the history of that period.) But this does not mean that if the historical details in the book are found to be reliable we may conclude that the book was written by Daniel or someone contemporary with him. Such a finding would indicate only that the book had been written by someone who had a good knowledge of the period, someone who might have lived at the time or in a later age. If this situation should arise we should have to find some other means of locating the writer in time.

On the other hand, if the historical data in the book do not reflect accurate knowledge of 6th-century Babylonian affairs — that is to say, if it is found to be quite wrong about such affairs, for it may be that slight divergences from what is known from the official records of Nebuchadnezzar, Cyrus, or whoever, may be allowed as representing a different, though still contemporary, point of view — it would follow that neither Daniel nor any contemporary of his wrote it. In such circumstances, too, we should then have to pursue the quest for the author of Daniel in other ways.

We must also, before we proceed, clarify what we mean when we refer to the "historical data" of the book of Daniel, because everything in the book is potentially historical. If the book was written by Daniel (or a contemporary), if the stories are "true", then every detail may be held to be historical. However, we cannot presume that this is the case; this is one of the things we are attempting to establish. We must, therefore, understand the term "historical data" in a restricted sense, we must understand it to mean data which we may reasonably expect to find in contemporary sources.

57

We may immediately identify several details in Daniel as not belonging to this class of "historical data". Daniel's private visions, for example, would not have been recorded in official Babylonian or Persian chronicles. Nebuchadnezzar's dream need not have been recorded in the official annals, since the incident was essentially a private affair. His madness it might not have been politic for the royal chroniclers to record, while Belshazzar's annalists would not have had time to record an account of the writing on the wall. Of these incidents, therefore, we shall take no account.

What about Nebuchadnezzar's erection of a statue, the worship of which was imposed on the entire population of his empire, or Darius's administrative reorganization, his creation of 120 satrapies under the jurisdication of three presidents, one of whom was on one occasion thrown to the lions but survived? The institution of both Nebuchadnezzar's religious and Darius's administrative reforms, if not their effect on the several Jewish civil servants of whom stories are told in the book of Daniel, would surely have been widely known and ought to have been recorded. These must thus qualify as "historical data", but contemporary sources are silent about both of them.

This silence may give rise to suspicions about the historicity of the incidents recorded in Daniel, but strictly speaking, for the purpose of our present investigation, it is, like the silence on those matters we have already decided not to be "historical data", not significant. It is always possible that the book of Daniel contains the only surviving record of certain incidents.

There are, in fact, only two elements in Daniel which can satisfy our requirements and qualify as "historical data" for the purpose of the present exercise. These are (i) the statement in Dan. 1:1 that Nebuchadnezzar, king of Babylon, besieged Jerusalem in the third year of the reign of King Jehoiakim of Judah, and (ii) the names and sequence of the powers and individual rulers with whom Daniel is said to have come in contact.

It has been observed in a commentary on Daniel that "the very first statement in chapter one can be shown to be inaccurate"[1]. This statement is perhaps over-dogmatic, but there is certainly a difficulty about the historical value of Dan. 1:1. We may say immediately that we know nothing of such a siege from any other source. Nebuchadnezzar's own records do not mention one. To say more we shall have to review that period in some detail.

Nebuchadnezzar succeeded his father Nabopolassar on the throne of Babylon in August 605 B.C., but his reign was officially reckoned, following Babylonian practice, to have begun at the New Year in 604. Jehoiakim came to the throne of Judah about September 609 B.C., having been installed there by Pharaoh Necho of Egypt, and

58

remained subservient to Egypt for the first four years of his reign. Egyptian dominance in Palestine was broken when they were defeated by Nebuchadnezzar at the battle of Carchemish in Syria in the summer (probably in May or June) of 605. Thus the earliest occasion on which the Babylonians could have invaded Judah was later in the summer of 605. Nebuchadnezzar was in that general area at the time but he was not then king of Babylon, while Jehoiakim was already in the fourth year of his reign. Thus the difficulty about the statement of Dan.1:1 is clear. However, it is perhaps not necessary to insist that Nebuchadnezzar should actually have been king at the time and there is a slim possibility that, as Alan Millard[2] has suggested, the battle of Carchemish and the period immediately after it, when Nebuchadnezzar "marched about victoriously" in the west, can be dated to Jehoiakim's third year.

To understand this suggestion we must consider some factors which frequently contribute to problems in chronology. In the ancient Near East two systems of reckoning years were used: the year might begin in spring or in autumn. The Babylonians used the former system, Judah (and Israel) probably used both systems at different times but there is no certainty about which system was in use at any given period. Further, there were two different methods of reckoning reigns. In one system, the ante-dating or non-accession year system, the first year of a ruler's reign was reckoned as the period from his accession to the end of that calendar year. This system was in use in Egypt. The other system, known as the post-dating or accession year system, was used in the Assyrian and neo-Babylonian empires. In this system the first year of a reign was that year which began at the New Year festival which followed the king's accession, the period between the accession and the following New Year being known as the king's accession year. It is not known which system was used in Judah: both systems may have been followed at different times.

Returning to the reign of Jehoiakim, we may say that *if* the year was reckoned in Judah in the late seventh century as beginning in the autumn, *and if* the accession year system was followed, *and if* Jehoiakim's accession was sufficiently late to necessitate the counting of almost a whole year as his accession year, then the battle of Carchemish and the period immediately after it would have been reckoned to Jehoiakim's third year.

The equation, made in Jer. 25:1, of Jehoiakim's fourth year with Nebuchadnezzar's first may be said to support the possibility thus envisaged. If Jer. 25:1 is using a precise and correct form for this dating, that is to say, if, by his reference to Nebuchadnezzar's first year he means his first year as reckoned officially in Babylon (i.e. 604 - 603, spring to spring), and if that was Jehoiakim's fourth year, then

Jehoiakim's third year could coincide with Nebuchadnezzar's accession year and an invasion of Judah by Nebuchadnezzar in the aftermath of Carchemish could legitimately be dated as it is in Dan. 1:1.

However, the possibility may not be discounted that Jeremiah is not using the correct Babylonian form of dating for Nebuchadnezzar, but in referring to Nebuchadnezzar's first year he is referring casually, or indeed correctly in accordance with the (different) Judaean system, to what was known in Babylon as his accession year. It may in fact appear likely that this is what Jeremiah is doing, for in Jer. 46:2 the battle of Carchemish is dated in the fourth year of Jehoiakim, that is, the same year which is equated in Jer. 25:1 with the first of Nebuchadnezzar. We know the date of Carchemish — summer 605 — and we know that that was not reckoned in Babylon as Nebuchadnezzar's first year, but since he acceded to the throne later in that year it could easily be called in a casual, non-technical way, his first year, the more so if the designation was being made by a Judaean who was familiar with a different system of reckoning reigns.

All this discussion may be reduced to a simple statement. Jer. 46:2 dates the battle of Carchemish in the fourth year of Jehoiakim, and Nebuchadnezzar could not have mounted an expedition against Judah before that battle. He could not, therefore, have besieged Jerusalem in Jehoiakim's third year and, we must say, the statement of Dan. 1:1 is at odds with the history of the period with which it purports to deal.

Turning now to the wider history of the period in which Daniel is represented as living, we may notice first that the book of Daniel mentions four successive rulers, Nebuchadnezzar and Belshazzar, his son, both of whom were Babylonians, Darius, who was a Mede, and Cyrus, a Persian. No indication is given of the length of any of their reigns, but that is not necessarily significant. The succession of rulers which actually took place was as follows: Nebuchadnezzar (604-562) was succeeded by his son Amel-marduk (561-560), who appears once or twice in the Old Testament as Evil-merodach. He was killed in a revolution and succeeded by his brother-in-law Ncriglissar (559-556), whose son Labashi-marduk followed him but was very shortly removed by a rebellion which resulted in Nabonidus, a nobleman from Harran, coming to the throne. Nabonidus's reign lasted from 555 until 539, when his kingdom was conquered by Cyrus. So, we have two very different pictures.

Now, of course Daniel does not have to have all the details; it is not a consecutive history and does not pretend to be one, but merely a selection of incidents from the life of Daniel. So we cannot say that the book of Daniel ought to mention Amel-marduk (or whomever) and hold the lack of mention to be a fault. But we can say that if Daniel knows kings not known to history it must raise doubts about the historical value of the book and about its having been written in Daniel's time.

What then do we do about the sequence of rulers? The non-mention in Daniel of Amel-marduk, Neriglissar, and so on, is not significant. But what about Belshazzar and Darius, who appear in Daniel?

To take Belshazzar first, it used to be said that there was no such person and that in mentioning him Daniel is totally unhistorical. While we may acknowledge that these conclusions were in their time entirely justified, it has been known since about 1850 that Nabonidus had a son, Belshazzar, who acted as regent in Babylon while he himself spent ten years at Teima in Arabia. On this basis it is often claimed that Daniel is after all historically accurate, but some important points must be noted. Belshazzar was not king; he is never called "king" in Babylonian documents, although one document does say that Nabonidus "entrusted the kingship to him" which shows that he had royal standing, yet he is regularly called "king" in Daniel. Secondly, Daniel treats Belshazzar as son of Nebuchadnezzar; he was not. The conclusion to which these observations lead is that, while the book of Daniel preserves the name of an historical individual which dropped out of the cognizance of historians for some two millennia, the inaccuracies which attend that figure would suggest that the stories in which he appears originated not contemporaneously with him but at some chronological remove.

The problem about Darius is that, while according to Daniel he reigned in Babylon for an unspecified period between Belshazzar and Cyrus (or, perhaps we should say, after Belshazzar and by implication before Cyrus), history allows no room for him. Babylon, ruled by Nabonidus (for whom Belshazzar acted as regent) was conquered by Cyrus.

The problem is not a new one. In the first century of this era it was recognized by Josephus, who said that Darius had another name amongst the Greeks. He did not, however, say what this "other name" was. It seems clear that Josephus, being aware that Darius the Mede was not known to history and being unwilling to assert that he must therefore be unhistorical, resorted to the only conclusion possible: that Darius must be someone who is known to history by another name; but he was unable to go any further. A number of people who have shared Josephus's premises have, in times ancient and modern, attempted to proceed further along the same path, and a number of suggestions have been made as to the identification of Darius.

One suggestion which was put forward at different times from the sixteenth century to the nineteenth is that Darius was really Nabonidus. In the period when Belshazzar was unknown to history this suggestion made a certain amount of sense. Nabonidus had long been known (he was known to historians in the classical period) as the last king of Babylon, the one conquered by Cyrus. If the unknown (outside Daniel) Belshazzar could be equated with Labashi-marduk (and this identification was made by some scholars) then, clearly, the Nabonidus who ousted Labashi-marduk in history would be the Darius who ousted Belshazzar in Daniel.

The suggestion is neat, so far as it goes, but an obvious question which may be raised against it is, how could Nabonidus, from Harran in western Mesopotamia, be Darius, the *Mede*? I have not gone back to the old books to find out how Grotius and his followers dealt with this question, which must surely have occurred to them, because, now that Belshazzar is known to have been Nabonidus's son the thesis is quite impossible.

It may be asked, might the case of Belshazzar (as it formerly existed) present a valuable parallel to the case of Darius? Belshazzar was once unknown to history and there was apparently no room to fit him in if he were known. That problem was resolved in what must have been a highly unexpected way, when he turned out to have been a regent acting for his father. Could Darius, similarly, have been a functionary of some kind who acted for Cyrus, so that whereas in the historical record Nabonidus gave way to Cyrus, in reality one deputy gave way to another? Did Cyrus have such a deputy?

As it happens, there is a candidate for the place, a figure whom I shall introduce by the Greek name Gobryas, a figure known from the historians Xenophon and Herodotus and also from various cuneiform documents from the time of Cyrus himself. It was Gobryas who led Cyrus's army into Babylon (without a fight), while Cyrus and his main army engaged the Babylonian forces at Opis on the Tigris. He became governor of Babylon and Trans-Euphrates and remained in that office throughout the reign of Cyrus and for at least the first five years of the reign of Cyrus's son and successor Cambyses. One of the first things that he did after taking office was to install subordinate governors in Babylon, an act which might be thought to echo the statement of Daniel chapter 6 that Darius appointed 120 satraps over the kingdom.

We may appear to have made a promising start on identifying Darius the Mede, who invaded Babylon on the night of Belshazzar's party and exercised authority there for an unspecified period, with Gobryas, but, unfortunately, the man I have just described never existed. "Gobryas", as I have described him, is an amalgam of at least two individuals whose names have both been represented by the same form — Gobryas — although they are different in the cuneiform texts, where they appear as Ugbaru and Gubaru. The man who entered Babylon at the head of Cyrus's army was Ugbaru. That incident occurred on 12th October 539. Ugbaru died on 6th November of the same year, which seems effectively to exclude him from further consideration. Apart from the question of whether all the events attributed in Daniel to the reign of Darius could be squeezed into three weeks, it is implicit in the date given in 9:1 and 11:1 — the first year of Darius — that he reigned for more than one year.

What about the other one; Gubaru, governor of Babylon throughout the reign of Cyrus and half of that of Cambyses? Can King Darius, son of Xerxes (Ahasuerus), the Mede, be equated with Gubaru, governor of Babylon, whose ancestry and nationality are unknown? There are some who certainly think so, but their arguments in favour of doing so are based solely on circumstantial evidence. Since we know nothing of Gubaru's family, he may well have been a Mede whose father was called Xerxes, but, it must be said, he may equally well not, and indeed the probability that he was not is infinitely greater than the possibility that he was.

The question centres on the names: Darius/Gubaru, and on the titles: king/governor. J.C. Whitcomb[3], who argues for the identification, suggests that Darius might have been an honorific title conferred on Gubaru, and that "king" might be a casual style of reference, in what is after all not an official document, to one who wielded enormous power.

If we ask the question, as we have above, "Can Darius be equated with Gubaru?", the answer will certainly be "Yes", because there is no evidence to the contrary. But it may be said — and said with perfect seriousness — that, on the same basis, Darius the Mede can be identified with Paddy McGinty's goat. However, if the question is put in a different, better, form, "Should Darius be equated with Gubaru?", or "Is there any basis for equating the two?", the answer must be a firm "No".

There is no earthly reason for saying that governor Gubaru and King Darius were one and the same. There is at least one weighty piece of evidence against the equation, and it applies also to other identifications of Darius — with Cambyses, son of Cyrus, who did rule for a time in Babylon as his father's deputy[4], or with Cyrus himself, as proposed by Wiseman[5] — and it is this:

If Darius is the same person as Gubaru, an official of Cyrus, the "reign" of Darius starts at the same point as that of Cyrus, and continues rather longer, for Gubaru is known to have outlived Cyrus. Thus the first year of Darius is the same as the first year of Cyrus, the second year of Cyrus is also the second year of Darius, and so on. Yet the writer of Daniel dates some events by the reign of Darius, some by the reign of Cyrus. The only reason he can have had for doing this is that he intended his references to the reign of Darius to be understood as relating to a period other than the reign of Cyrus.

The writer of Daniel clearly thought there was a Median king Darius who ruled Babylon between Belshazzar and Cyrus. Since history allows no room for such a figure we must pronounce the stories in which he appears to be fictitious. Not only that but, noting that references to Darius occur in the visions of Daniel at 9:1 and 11:1 — squarely in the visions and not in the introductory headings which may be attributed to an editor — we must conclude that these are not genuine accounts recorded in the sixth century B.C. by the man who experienced them.

Notes

[1]   N. Porteous, *Daniel. A Commentary* (London, 1965) p. 25.

[2]   A. Millard, "Daniel 1-6 and History", *Evangelical Quarterly* 49.2 (1977) p. 68f.

[3]   J.C. Whitcomb, *Darius the Mede* (Grand Rapids, 1974).

[4]   For this and other suggested identifications see H.H. Rowley, *Darius the Mede and the Four World Empires in the Book of Daniel* (Cardiff, 1964).

[5]   D.J. Wiseman, "Some historical problems in the book of Daniel", in D.J. Wiseman, *et al., Notes on some problems in the book of Daniel* (London, 1970).

Chapter 7

Daniel's Future

We must now turn to examine that part of the book of Daniel which looks ahead of the time in which Daniel is represented as living[1], and ask what the book says about this period and what that tells us about the book. Chapters 7-12 are devoted to Daniel's own visions of the future, but we must also consider in this context chapter 2, in which Nebuchadnezzar's dream is interpreted by Daniel as indicating that after Nebuchadnezzar would come in succession three other kingdoms and, finally, another kingdom, set up by God, which would never be destroyed.

There is nothing in this chapter to make the identification of these kingdoms obvious. It is not even immediately clear whether the term "kingdoms" in this context should be understood as referring to different imperial powers or to a succession of individual rulers, whether in one empire or in more than one. The former may seem the more obvious significance, probably simply because the use of the word "kingdom" might appear to imply this, but other words, such as "kingship", "rule" or "reign" might legitimately be substituted for it. The top tier of the statue is said to represent Nebuchadnezzar himself (2:37f.) and this might imply that the other parts of the statue should be taken to represent individual rulers too.

It may be tempting at this point to apply our knowledge of the history of the period from Nebuchadnezzar onwards in an attempt to establish the precise application of Nebuchadnezzar's dream. However, I think that, although it will eventually become necessary to do something like this, it would be wrong to do so at this point because too hasty a conclusion about what a passage means may cloud our judgement about what it says. What a passage says must always be the starting-point, and what Daniel chapter 2 says is that Nebuchadnezzar *is* the first in a series of four successive powers, which are characterized as, respectively, gold, silver, bronze and iron (with an admixture of clay in the iron at the end), and that all of these powers will be superseded by a divinely established and everlasting kingdom.

That said, let us leave chapter two for the moment and turn our attention to Daniel's visions in chapters 7-12. We can take these in the order in which they occur in the book.

In chapter 7 Daniel's vision is first recounted and then the explanation of the vision, which is given to Daniel by a bystander in the vision, follows. A succession of four fearsome beasts represents a succession of four kingdoms. That these kingdoms are different imperial powers seems certain, since the fourth beast has ten horns which represent ten kings (v.24). There is also an eleventh horn, a little horn, which displaces three others. That is, an eleventh king, who does away with three other kings, who plans "to alter the customary times and law" (v.25), who makes war on the saints and triumphs over them for a period expressed cryptically as "a time and times (perhaps, two times) and half a time", until judgement is given against him in a court presided over by one "Ancient in Years" and then the saints set up an everlasting kingdom.

To some extent this appears to parallel Nebuchadnezzar's dream in chapter 2. The essential details of either chapter could be summarized in a statement such as this: a succession of four empires is brought to an end and an everlasting kingdom is set up. May we conclude, then, that the two chapters are dealing with the same events and, incidentally, that the "kingdoms" of chapter 2 must be empires as in chapter 7, and not the reigns of individual kings? Conversely, we may ask, is there any obstacle to making this identification?

In the absence of any argument to the contrary, it seems reasonable to conclude that chapters 2 and 7 are dealing with the same events, with chapter 7 giving more details, particularly with respect to the fourth kingdom. But despite all the details nothing is yet made explicit about the identity of the kingdoms or kings, such as the little horn. Again, it is tempting to go beyond the book of Daniel, to history, to look for an imperial power which might be represented as, say, a lopsided bear with three ribs in its mouth (number two of the series) or for an individual whose activities might correspond with those of the little horn, but again I counsel restraint, on the same grounds as before. We must wait until we have exhausted all the information in the book before we go further afield. Let us content ourselves with noting what chapter 7 says (we shall worry later about what it means) and move on to chapter 8.

In chapter 8 we find a second vision of Daniel, dated two years after that of chapter 7. In this vision a ram is attacked and mauled by a goat. The goat has a single horn which unaccountably breaks and is replaced by four horns. Out of one of these grows a little horn. During the ascendancy of this little horn the sanctuary is destroyed and the daily offering is suspended for a period of 2300 evenings and mornings, after which "the Holy Place shall emerge victorious" (v.14).

The vision is explained to Daniel by a personage called Gabriel, who appears in the semblance of a man (which implies that he is not one) in the course of the vision. The ram, Daniel is told, symbolizes the Medo-Persian empire; the goat is the Greek empire, and the great horn on its forehead is its first king. Thus far, we have simply repeated what is stated explicitly in the text, but here we have a pretty clear identification which allows us to step out of the confines of what we are actually told. We can confidently name the great horn of the goat as Alexander.

The four horns, then are the *Diadochoi*, or successors to Alexander, and the little horn is a king of one of the four successor states, carved by them out of Alexander's empire after his death. Granted this much information, it might now appear a relatively easy matter to reach a conclusion about the identity of this ruler, but let us not be too hasty. There are other questions which must be asked first. For one, we may ask ourselves whether it is legitimate to equate this little horn with the little horn of chapter 7. The fact that the same symbol is employed in both places would appear to be a reasonable starting point for such an equation. The activities of the two little horns, as they are described in the two chapters, are similar, although it may be acknowledged that nowhere are these described in precisely identical terms. Still, when we find the first little horn hurling defiance at the Most High and holding the saints in thrall, and the second aspiring to be as great as the Prince of the Host, suppressing the regular offering, and trampling the Holy Place underfoot, must we not conclude that the same situation is being described in two different ways? Above all, we must note that the vision of chapter 8 is said repeatedly to relate to the time of the end, while in chapter 7 the reign of the little horn is followed by the new kingdom in which the people of the saints of the Most High are to hold everlasting power.

If we identify (and we must) the little horn of chapter 8 with that of chapter 7 we can now go back and tidy up the question of the four empires. If the little horn of chapter 8 represents a Hellenistic king, and the same person is represented by the little horn of chapter 7, then the fourth beast in chapter 7 must be the Greek empire.

The description (Dan.7:7) of that beast — "dreadful and grisly, exceedingly strong, with great iron teeth and bronze claws. It crunched and devoured, and trampled underfoot all that was left" — fits Alexander's military machine which rolled across the Near East, from Greece to India, in a few years. Although it must be acknowledged that it could also fit other imperial powers, there is one detail which does seem particularly appropriate as a reference to the

Greeks (apart, of course, from the little horn, which is the basis of the identification), and that is the simple, almost trivial, remark that this beast "was different from all the others" (vv. 7, 19). The Greek empire was certainly different from its predecessors in a fundamental sense. All the preceding powers had their base in the East — in Mesopotamia (Assyria, Babylon) or next door, in Iran (Persia, Media). Residents of, say, Palestine would scarcely have noticed any changes in the century or so that saw the transition from Assyrian to Babylonian to Persian domination. Aramaic remained the common *lingua franca*, for example. But the Greeks, from Europe, brought a totally different culture and the world changed dramatically.

If the fourth beast is Greece then the fourth kingdom in chapter 2 must also be Greece, for we have already seen that chapters 2 and 7 seem to reflect the same scheme of four successive powers. Well, that's all right. The iron part of the statue represents Greece: iron for Alexander, iron and clay mixed in the toes for the successor states, perhaps. I would not press these suggestions, for chapter 2 appears not to be concerned very much with details. The main point is the sequence gold — silver — bronze — iron. However, one point does strike a chord; the reference to mingling together in marriage (2:43) brings to mind Alexander's policy of uniting the world through intermarriage and his practice of holding mass marriage ceremonies for his troops and local women.

So, the fourth kingdom is Greece, the first is Babylon (since in 2:37f Nebuchadnezzar is said to be represented by the head of the statue); that leaves numbers two and three to be identified. According to the book of Daniel, the last Babylonian ruler, Belshazzar, was followed by Darius the Mede, who was in turn followed by Cyrus the Persian, so kingdom number two must be Media, and number three Persia.

It is possible that an objection may be made to this identification on the basis that Dan. 8 treats the kingdom of the Medes and the Persians as a single entity (represented there by the ram) and that the writer would not, therefore, have represented as two separate entities (in the four kingdom sequence) what he knew to have been one entity.

This objection has indeed been made, but there may be a fallacy inherent in it. Let us, in the first place, illuminate the point with a simple analogy. If we ask, "Would the use of the term "Great Britain" in one chapter of a book preclude the author of that book from referring to England and Scotland as separate entities in another chapter?", the answer would have to be that it would, if it was implied that Great Britain had never been anything but a United Kingdom (or, *vice versa*, if it was implied that England and Scotland had nothing in common but their border, the use of the term "Great

Britain" would be excluded). So, if the description of the Medo-Persian empire as a unit (as in chapter 8) implies that it had never been anything but one unit, the objection may be sustained. We must now ask, what does chapter 8 say or imply about the relationship between the Medes and the Persians?

First, it *says* (v.20), "the two-horned ram . . . signifies the kings of Media and Persia". Apparently, the duality in the kingdom is symbolized by the two horns. Further, we are told (v.3) that the two horns were long, one was longer than the other, and the longer one came up "behind" or "later". This is not explained in the chapter, but it might be taken to indicate that the power which was dominant at first (the first horn) was superseded by the second half of the duality (the second horn, growing up after the first and overtaking it).

Historically speaking, the Medes and the Persians were two related peoples living in Iran. At the time of their emergence in history, in the seventh century B.C., the Medes were the dominant power in Iran, and the Persians were subservient to them, but the balance of power was reversed by Cyrus. Cyrus, in the first place, was vassal king of Anshan (Persia) under Astyages of Media (his maternal grandfather). In 550 he rebelled, with support from Nabonidus of Babylon, and thereafter the Persians were dominant, although they continued to use the dual term, Medes and Persians. Thus, there is no incompatibility between describing the Medes and Persians as a single entity, on the one hand, and as two separate entities, on the other. It is not, historically speaking, inaccurate to speak of a Median (or, as we might put it, a Medo-persian) empire, as distinct from a Persian (or Perso-median) one.

It is, of course, true that the internal shift in the balance of power within Iran had taken place before the conquest of Babylon and that the sequence Babylon — Media — Persia — Greece, as a chronological sequence of imperial powers, is therefore unhistorical. This conclusion will have implications for our final judgement on the nature of the book of Daniel, but our immediate objective has been to identify the four kingdoms and we have done that from within the book of Daniel itself. We may now continue our survey of Daniel's future.

In chapter 9 we find Daniel pondering on Jeremiah's pronouncement that Jerusalem was to remain in ruins for 70 years. The reference is probably to Jer. 25:11ff, or it may be to Jer. 29:10. The former passage reads,

> "For seventy years this whole country shall be a scandal and a horror; these nations shall be in subjection to the king of Babylon. When those seventy years are completed, I will punish

the king of Babylon and his people . . . they will be the victims of mighty nations and great kings . . ."

the latter,

"When a full seventy years has passed over Babylon, I will take up your cause and fulfil the promise of good things I made you, by bringing you back to this place".

Daniel, pondering on one or both of these passages, is told by Gabriel that "70 years" really means 70 weeks of years, i.e. 490 years. At the end of this period, "rebellion shall be stopped, sin brought to an end, iniquity expiated, everlasting right ushered in, vision and prophecy sealed, and the Most Holy Place anointed" (v.24).

After a brief reference to an event occurring relatively early in this time scale — the appearance at the end of seven "weeks" (i.e. 49 years) of an anointed prince — attention is focussed on the last seven years, the 70th "week" of the scheme. Then, Daniel is told,

"one who is anointed shall be removed with no one to take his part; and the horde of an invading prince shall work havoc on city and sanctuary. The end of it shall be a deluge, inevitable war with all its horrors. He shall make a firm league with the mighty/many for one week; and, the week half spent, he shall put a stop to sacrifice and offering." (v.26f.)

There is a fair measure of detail here and, particularly in view of the chronological information, it may appear at least potentially simple to work out the application of the passage, but there is nothing obvious stated in it. That is to say, there is nothing in it of the kind of thing we have found in chapter 8, where it *says* the goat is Greece and the ram Persia. There may even be some question about the date from which the reckoning of the 490 years should start.

The statement in Dan. 9:25, "from the the time that the word went forth that Jerusalem should be restored and rebuilt", which marks the beginning of the period, might prompt one to think of the edict of Cyrus, issued in his first year, which authorized the restoration of the city. On this view the reckoning would start in 538/7 and end in 48/7 B.C. However, in the first year of Darius, when the event of Dan. 9 is dated, the reign of Cyrus still lay in the future, and it would seem highly improbable that Daniel should be told not only that the 70 years of which Jeremiah spoke should be understood to mean 490 years but that this span of time had yet to begin. The "word" in question has to be that spoken by Jeremiah, in which he was talking about the exile of the Jews in Babylon and envisaged a period of 70 years from the time he spoke. To re-interpret the reference to "70 years" as actually meaning "490 years" is one thing, but it is quite another to suggest that the 490 should start only when the 70 ended; to suggest, in other words, that when Jeremiah said "70", meaning "490", he really intended "560".

The 490 years must surely start at the same time as Jeremiah's 70, but when was that? The final destruction of Jerusalem occurred in 587. Should we reckon from then, and find the climax in 97 B.C.? Or should we, rather, insist that "from the time that the word went forth" in Dan. 9:25 should point us firmly to the date on which Jeremiah uttered his words as the starting point?

If we follow this latter approach we shall find that we still have a choice of dates, for Jer. 29, in which a letter from the prophet to a group of exiles in Babylon is recorded, must be dated sometime after 597, the year in which King Jehoiachim was deported — the date 594 is widely assigned to that letter — but Jer. 25, in which the prophet first spoke of the 70-year domination of Babylon, is dated in the fourth year of Jehoiakim, 605 B.C. 490 years on from these dates will take us to 115 B.C., in the latter case, or to 107, or even 104 B.C. in the former.

There is no basis for choosing one route rather than another and, this being so, it might be tempting to take each of the possibilities in turn, to calculate not only the termination date but also the intervening dates (the end of the 7th and 69th weeks), and then to test each set of dates against what we know of the history of the period and so decide which set it is appropriate to use. However, I would suggest, as I have already done in similar situations, that this is not the right way to proceed. Before attempting to pin down the application of chapter 9 in this way we should first make sure we have exhausted all the data in the book. In other words, we must first go on to examine chapters 10-12 and see what we find there, and then we can return to the details of chapter 9.

Nevertheless, two things may be noted at this point. First, the chronological scheme of Daniel 9 looks as though it reaches its climax at the end of the second century B.C. (somewhere between 115 and 97 B.C.). These dates fall within the period of the Hellenistic "successor" states, the period to which chapter 8 pointed. The second point is the statement of 9:27 that for half of the last "week", i.e. for $3\frac{1}{2}$ years, sacrifice and offering would be stopped. We have already found a reference to the cessation of sacrifice, in Dan. 8:14, where it is said the regular offering (in the temple) would be suppressed for 2300 evenings and mornings, which is equivalent to 1150 days, or 3 years and 2 or 3 months, depending on whether a year is reckoned as having

365 days (solar year) or 354 (lunar year). Is this near enough to 3½ years, which may well be intended as an approximation rather than a specific statement of time, to enable us to say that the two places which refer to sacrifice being stopped are talking about the same incident? Can we further suggest that the cryptic statement of 7:25, "a time and times, and half a time", the period during which the little horn triumphed over the saints, should be understood as referring to the same 3½ year period?

If so, then the "invading prince" of 9:26 must be the "little horn" of chapters 7 and 8, and we can see, if we review chapters 7 and 8, along with chapter 9, that the same events are being alluded to in each successive vision, the picture gradually becoming clearer at each stage. In chapter 7, the "little horn", an unidentified ruler of an unnamed empire, triumphs over the "saints" temporarily, for three and a half periods of time, but the saints are victorious in the end and win an everlasting kingdom. In chapter 8, the "little horn" is located in history as a king in one of the Greek successor states. He will cause the suspension of sacrifice for three years and a bit. In chapter 9, the same events are given a more or less precise date, which appears to be about the end of the second century B.C.

Before we can proceed any further towards pinning down these events in history, we must see what further information is provided by the writer of the book. Let us turn, then to the last of Daniel's visions, in chapters 10-12.

In this last vision a supernatural visitor, who is described only as "a man" but is apparently the same Gabriel who appears in chapter 9, explains to Daniel in clear language events in the future leading up to the time of the end. Chapter 10 forms an introduction in which the man appears and the scene is set; chapters 11-12 contain his account of the future. Since the account is "in clear", i.e. not expressed symbolically, we could deal with it straight off, from the top down, but it might be better to do this in two stages. First, we shall make a broad survey of the contents of the chapter, picking out a few details to see the perspective of the whole, and then we shall look at the whole passage in greater detail.

The vision is dated in the third year of Cyrus (10:1). In that year Daniel is told (11:2) that there are to be three more kings in Persia and the fourth (whether this is to be understood as the fourth reckoning from Cyrus or his fourth successor, is a question to which we shall have to return) will "rouse the whole world against the kingdom of Greece". Thereafter (vv. 3, 4) will appear a warrior king who will rule a vast kingdom and do what he chooses, but as soon as he is established his kingdom will be shattered ... it will not pass to his descendants ... [but] will be given to others as well as to them.

This seems clearly to refer to Alexander the Great who, within ten years of his accession to the throne of Macedonia, established an empire which reached to India (destroying the Persian empire in the process) but died a few years later at the height of his power, aged 33. After his death his empire broke up into four main parts, in which power was seized by his generals: Thrace and Asia Minor were held by Lysimachus; Macedonia by Cassander; Egypt by Ptolemy; and Syria by Seleucus.

The dynasties founded by the last two of these (the Ptolemies and the Seleucids) held sway, each in turn, over Palestine, and so the book of Daniel focusses on the two dynasties, the Kings of the North (the Seleucid rulers of Syria) and the Kings of the South (the Ptolemies of Egypt). Vv. 5-20 outline the doings of two rival rulers over several generations. If we take a quick glance over this material we see that, after the first King of the North (v. 6ff), there is a reference to "his sons" (v. 10), a new "king of the North" appears in v.20, and there is a further stage in the series at v.21, when a "contemptible creature" comes on the scene, whose doings occupy the rest of the chapter (25 verses).

At v.31 we find a statement which has a familiar ring.

"Armed forces dispatched by him will desecrate the sanctuary and the citadel and do away with the regular offering".

Already in 9:26ff, we have had a reference to someone putting a stop to sacrifice and offering, and in 8:11 the little horn of that vision

"aspired to be as great as the Prince of the host, suppressed his regular offering and even threw down his sanctuary".

We have already seen that the "little horn" of chapters 7 and 8 can be identified with the "invading prince" of 9:26. Now, in 11:21, he is described as

"a contemptible creature ... [who] will seize the kingdom by dissimulation in time of peace".

Who is this? At last we face the question squarely and in the expectation that, if we retrace our steps to the beginning of chapter 11 and follow the unfolding history of the passage, we shall be led to the answer.

After Alexander's empire broke up in the manner already described, Ptolemy, in Egypt, was the dominant power. The book of

Daniel, speaking of events in the future, says "the King of the South will become strong" (11:5). The same verse continues,

> "but another of the captains will surpass him in strength and win a greater kingdom".

Seleucus, who was at first satrap of Babylonia but displaced by Antigonus, the satrap of Phrygia, served under Ptolemy for a few years before re-establishing himself. He subsequently extended his power to embrace the major part of Alexander's empire, and ruled a territory which extended from Asia Minor to the northwest frontier of India.

Dan. 11:6 predicts the making of an alliance between the kings of the North and the South, cemented by the marriage of a daughter of the King of the South to the King of the North, but "she and her escort, her child, and also her lord and master, will all be the victims of foul play". Ptolemy II (285-246) gave his daughter Berenice in marriage to Antiochus II (261-247), the third Seleucid ruler. Berenice and her child, and Antiochus, too, were all murdered at the instigation of Antiochus's first wife.

This happened about 248 B.C. and Ptolemy II died soon afterwards, and so we find in Dan. 11:7 "another shoot from the same stock as hers" appearing in her father's place. Berenice's brother succeeded his father as Ptolemy III (246-221), and he mounted a successful invasion of Seleucid territory (vv.7, 8). Seleucus II (247-226) attempted a counter-invasion of Egypt in 244 but met with only partial success (v.9). Seleucus was succeeded by two of his sons in turn, Seleucus III (226-223) and Antiochus III [the Great] (223-187), hence the reference to "his sons" in Dan. 11:10.

Up to this time Palestine had been ruled by the Ptolemies. Antiochus III moved southward in 219, scoring military successes and reaching as far as Gaza (the "stronghold" of v.10). At the battle of Raphia (217), Ptolemy IV routed Antiochus's army but did not follow up this victory (vv. 11ff), and "when the years come [came] round" (v.13), in 203, Antiochus returned to the attack and at the battle of Panion, in 198, he finally wrested control of Palestine from the Ptolemies. As Dan. 11:16 puts it, he established (Daniel has the future tense, of course) himself "in the fairest of all lands and it [came] wholly into his power".

After this, Antiochus turned his attention towards Greece, making a series of expeditions between 196 and 191, but the Romans intervened and Antiochus was defeated, retreated homewards and died soon afterwards (v.18f).

The reign of his successor is encapsulated in Dan. 11:20.

"One who will send out an officer with a royal escort to extort tribute; after a short time this king too will meet his end, yet neither openly nor in battle".

Seleucus IV (187-175), the son and successor of Antiochus III, sent his chief minister Heliodorus to raid the temple treasury at Jerusalem. The incident is reported in II Maccabees 3. He was assassinated by the same Heliodorus and was succeeded by his brother Antiochus IV (175-164) who is, thus, the "contemptible creature" of Dan. 11:21, to whose reign the rest of the chapter is devoted.

Antiochus's succession was, in the first place, illegitimate, as Dan. 11:21 recognizes. The rightful heir was the son of Seleucus IV, Demetrius, who was living in Rome as a hostage for his father's good behaviour, but Antiochus seized the throne after his brother's death. His career, as it is outlined in Daniel 11, falls into three parts, each of which includes a campaign against Egypt (the King of the South).

The first of these took place in 169 (v.25ff). While Antiochus was engaged on this campaign in Egypt, the rumour spread in Jerusalem that he was dead, and a former High Priest, Jason, who had once been the protegee of Antiochus before he had been displaced by a higher bidder for the office, attempted to recover his old office. Antiochus was far from dead and, returning from Egypt, he visited Jerusalem with retribution for the rebellion. He plundered the temple and massacred the inhabitants of the city (see I Macc. 1).

In the following year (168) Antiochus mounted his second invasion of Egypt (v.29ff). This invasion was shortlived and Antiochus returned humiliated, after being chased out of Egypt by the Roman ambassador C. Papillius Laenas ("ships from Kittim", Dan. 11:30). Again he turned on Jerusalem and, according to I Macc. 1, sacked the city, massacred many of its inhabitants and installed a garrison of his troops in the citadel near the temple, where it was to remain for a long time. On top of this, Antiochus interfered with Jewish religious practices.

In his favour it must be said that he was not just "anti-semitic". His policy was one of uniting his diverse empire in one common culture, the Hellenistic culture, and so he opposed all local religions, intending to replace them with one, the worship of Zeus, with himself as the human manifestation of Zeus, Theos Epiphanes. We may recall here that the writer of Daniel denounces him for ignoring his own ancestral gods and the "god beloved of women" (Tammuz) (11:37) as much as for his persecutions of the Jews.

I Macc. 1:41ff gives details of Antiochus's edict banning the practice of the Jewish religion: the sacrificial ritual was to be suspended; the sabbath and festivals were no longer to be observed;

circumcision was no longer to be practised; possession of a book of Torah was banned; pagan altars were to be erected and pigs and other animals which the Jews would consider to be ritually unclean were to be offered in sacrifice. The climax came on 15th Kislev 167 (the date is given in I Macc. 1:54), when a structure, called by the writers of both Daniel and Maccabees the "Abomination of Desolation", was erected in the temple at Jerusalem. This was an altar and statue of Zeus; its name is a pun on the Hebrew appellation "Lord of Heaven" which was used to designate Zeus. Ten days after its erection, on 25th Kislev 167, the first pagan sacrifice was offered on it. This situation, reflected in Dan. 11:30-39, provided the spark which ignited the Maccabaean rebellion — which is perhaps referred to in 11:34, as the "little help" which is to be available to those fighting against persecution.

On 25th Kislev 164, after the initial successes of his rebellion, Judas Maccabaeus rededicated the temple, but the book of Daniel says nothing about that. It tells us, rather, about a third military campaign of Antiochus IV against Egypt (v. 40ff) in which Antiochus, initially victorious, was to withdraw after hearing "rumours from east and north" (v.44) and, encamping in Palestine, between Jerusalem and the sea, would "meet his end with no one to help him" (v.45), when "Michael the great captain, who stands guard over [the Jews]" (12:1) would appear to vindicate their cause.

None of this happened. The third Egyptian campaign never took place. In 165 Antiochus set off on a campaign in the east, in Persia, from which he never returned. About the time that the Jews were rededicating the temple in Jerusalem, in December 164, he died, probably of natural causes although I Macc. 6 says he died of grief on hearing of the successes of the Jewish rebels.

These last few observations, that the book of Daniel knows of the erection of the "Abomination of Desolation", which occurred in December 167, but not of its removal, which happened in December 164, and offers an account of Antiochus's last military campaign which is rather different from the one on which he actually came to the end of his life, have significant implications for the answer to our basic question about the nature of the book of Daniel and the date at which it was composed. However, before we explore these implications it will be necessary for us to take up some matters which have previously been left to one side. These are the chronological scheme of chapter 9 and the Persian rulers referred to in 11:2.

To take the latter matter first, according to Dan. 11:2, in the third year of Cyrus Daniel is told that there are to be three more kings in Persia and "the fourth", who will be far richer than all of them, "will rouse the whole world against the kingdom of Greece". Now, aside from the question of the identity of these kings, two questions arise here: (a) how many kings are intended? Is "the fourth" to be understood as the fourth ruler, reckoning Cyrus as the first, or the fourth successor of Cyrus, that is, another one in addition to the three successors specified? (b) Why are only four, or five, Persian kings indicated, when there were eleven in all, not counting the odd usurper?

It may appear that the obvious way to deal with question (a) is to look to the actual sequence of Persian rulers in order to settle the question. In similar cases encountered formerly there was good reason to hold back but that is not so here. There is no further information to be gleaned from the book. However the procedure is not quite so simple as it may appear, for the sequence of Persian rulers is this:

Cyrus (538-529)
Cambyses (529-522)
[Gaumata (522)]
Darius I (521-486)
Xerxes (486-465)
Artaxerxes I (465-424)
Xerxes II (423)
Darius II (423-404)
Artaxerxes II (404-358)
Artaxerxes III (358-338)
Arses (338-336)
Darius III (336-331)

When we look at this list we find that we have not just one problem but two: should the usurper Gaumata be reckoned as a king? The fourth king *after* Cyrus could be either Xerxes or Artaxerxes I, depending on whether Gaumata is or is not brought into the reckoning. The fourth king reckoning Cyrus as the first could be either Darius I or Xerxes, depending on the same consideration.

Xerxes, who mounted an invasion of Greece which ended in his defeat at Salamis in 480 B.C., may appear to be a promising candidate for being the fourth king, who roused the whole world against Greece, but to jump to the conclusion that a reference to him was intended would be false exegesis in that it involves reasoning from Xerxes backwards and not forwards from Daniel. (The fact that the name of Xerxes appears as one possible answer on the basis of either system of counting is of course without significance, although such an observation may appear important in a system of logic beloved by advertisers.) In any case, it still would not lead us to an answer to the question of why only four or five kings are indicated.

Let us then tackle the other question, but in an indirect way. We have discovered already that the book of Daniel is not accurate in reporting 6th-century history, but it is accurate in its description of events of the third and second centuries (down to 167). This allows the conclusion to be drawn that the book was actually written in the second century, in fact, shortly after 167. Supposing for a moment that this was actually the case, what better explanation could there be for the mention of four kings out of eleven than that the writer knew only of the existence of four Persian rulers? The Old Testament knows the names of only four Persian kings — Cyrus, Darius, Xerxes, Artaxerxes. Darius II and, perhaps, Artaxerxes II are referred to but not distinguished from the first of the name(s), who also appear, and the unsuspecting bible-reader might well conclude that only four kings are mentioned or even that only four ever existed. The most satisfactory solution to the problem of the reference in Daniel to only four out of eleven Persian rulers (and it would appear on this approach to have been four that was intended and not five) is the supposition that the writer of the book (or of that part of it), being dependent for his knowledge of the Persian period on the Old Testament, surmised that the four names recorded there indicated four kings and had no reason to think there ever had been any others.

Returning, now, to chapter nine, in which the prophecy of Jeremiah that Jerusalem was to remain in ruins for 70 years (at least according to Daniel's version of it) is interpreted by Gabriel as referring to a period of 490 years (70 weeks of years), we find that the period in question is to be divided in three parts, thus:

7 weeks,	i.e. 49 years	
62 weeks,	i.e. 434 years	
1 week,	i.e. 7 years,	this period being divided in two halves, each of $3\frac{1}{2}$ years.

When we looked at this passage earlier, we observed that while there may be some difficulty about the starting-point for this chronological sequence the end of it is apparently somewhere around the end of the second century B.C. (115/4 at the earliest; 97 at the latest). But when we traced the developments of chapter 11, we found "the time of the end" was being predicted there for sometime in the reign of Antiochus IV (175-164/3), in fact sometime after December 167. 490 years earlier would be 657-654, but these dates are impossibly early. They are long before Jeremiah's birth, and some 70 years before the destruction of Jerusalem. What, then, do we do about Daniel 9?

If we look again at the chart given above we may notice two things.

First, the three periods are by no means equal in length. The third is quite short, in terms of human experience, the first is of manageable length, but the middle period is quite unconscionably long. Secondly, very few details are offered about events in this long expanse of time, only two events, in fact, are mentioned. One occurs at the end of the first period when "one anointed, a prince", appears; the other marks the beginning of the final seven years, when "one who is anointed shall be removed with no one to take his part". Patently, the anointed one is not the same individual in both cases.

Now, further, it is said in 9:27 that, halfway through the last week "he shall put a stop to sacrifice and offering", and this we can date to December 167. So, for the beginning of that "week" we must go back three and a half years, to mid-170, and what do we find? In that year Onias III, the last Zadokite priest of the Jerusalem temple, was murdered. "An anointed one shall be removed with no one to take his part". Are we on the right track?

Let us go back to the other end, to the first 49 years. The most obvious place to begin the reckoning is 587, the date of the destruction of Jerusalem. 49 years later was 538, the first year of Cyrus's reign as reckoned officially in Babylon. If that was the year of "the appearance of one anointed, a prince" who could this have been but Cyrus himself? He was a prince, certainly, and he is designated Yahweh's anointed in Isa. 45:1. Alternatively, the same period saw the restoration of the priesthood of Jerusalem after the exile, with Joshua as the first High Priest. Either of these two candidates would fit the bill; both have their supporters.

We are left, thus, with 62 "weeks", that is, 434 years to span the period from 538 to 170, which was actually only 368 years long. So we may conclude that the writer of Daniel 9 had a detailed knowledge of the chronology of the beginning and end of his period but did not know the chronology of the intervening part correctly. However, he wanted to impose a chronological scheme on the period and he did this as best he could.

Note on Ideas of Chronology in Antiquity

Ignorance of the chronology of the Persian period (which is what is involved here) is not unique to the writer of Daniel. The *Damascus Document* from Qumran dates the origin of the community 390 years after Nebuchadnezzar's destruction of Jerusalem, which probably indicates an error of about 20 years (on the low side) in the reckoning of the sectarians. The Jewish chronographer Demetrius in the third century B.C. reckoned the period from the destruction of Jerusalem in 587 to the accession of Ptolemy IV in 221 as 338 years, i.e. 28 years short of the actual 366. On the other hand, Josephus reckoned as 481 (in the *Antiquities*) and 471 (in the *War*) years the period between the return from the exile in 538 and the death of Aristobulus I in 103 B.C. — too long a period in either case. (The most extreme example of the lack of chronological sense in antiquity must be Josephus' assigning the composition of all the Old Testament books to the "3000 years between Moses and Artaxerxes I".) Finally, we may notice the chronology drawn up by R. Yose the Galilean in *Seder Olam Rabah* in the second century A.D. The period between the destruction of Jerusalem by the Babylonians (587 B.C.) and its destruction by the Romans (A.D. 70) he judged to be 490 years, a figure which he undoubtedly derived from Daniel, which he allocated to the various powers as follows:

Babylonians	70 years	(actually 48 or 49)
Persians	34 years	(actually *ca.* 210)
Greeks	180 years	(approx. correct; from Alexander to Simon's independence)
Hasmonaeans	103 years	(about right: 142 (Simon) — 40 (Herod).)
Herodians	103 years	(a little low; at least 107. 110 needed if Hasmonaean period not to be adjusted.)

Starting with 490 years in view he probably worked back as far as Alexander with reasonable accuracy, took the 70 years for the Babylonians from Jeremiah, and was left with 34 years into which to fit the Persians.

Notes

[1] In this chapter all those periods to which Daniel's predictions relate will be considered as "Daniel's Future", although Daniel is represented as living through some of those periods and there is thus an area of overlap with his "Life and Times".

Chapter 8

The Book of Daniel is ...

It is time now to tackle squarely the fundamental question to which we have addressed ourselves and towards which we have been working in our enquiry into what the book of Daniel says about the history of the period covered in it. The question is, What is the book of Daniel? What kind of book is it, when was it written, and why?

We have made one important discovery in our examination of the book. We have established that the time envisaged as the "time of the end" was in the middle of 163 B.C., that is three and a half years after the suspension of sacrifice which took place in December 167. We have thus discovered the date of the book's publication — it was to be sealed until the time of the end — and also, therefore, the latest possible date for its composition. In principle, it could have been written at any time before then, shortly beforehand or 400 years earlier (i.e. by Daniel). In other words, the account of "Daniel's future" could be either history written in the guise of prediction or genuine prediction made by Daniel. How is the choice between the two possibilities to be made?

Taking the broad view, considering the book as a whole, the appearance in it of the unhistorical Darius the Mede means that it could not have been written by Daniel. But suppose the book is a collection of documents, as may be implied by the clear distinction which has been observed between the different parts, the stories and the visions, and perhaps especially by the fact that the accounts in the first person singular are introduced by short passages written in the third person; in such a case, might the visions (recorded in the first person) have been written by Daniel? May they be treated as genuine visions?

It is sometimes suggested that those who hold that the book was composed at a late date (i.e. in the second century B.C.) do so because they deny the possibility of Daniel's having received divine revelations. I do not know whether anybody really has ever denied this possibility. I have never encountered such a denial, and I am not going to make one myself. It is certainly possible that Daniel, in the sixth century B.C., should have received divine revelations and written a record of them. The question which we have to answer is, is it reasonable to think that he did?

Let us consider some implications of the proposition that in the visions of Daniel we have a genuine record, written by Daniel, of visions experienced by him. On the supposition that Daniel's visions were genuine divine revelations, how can we account for their errors in (a) seeing four imperial powers where there were only three (the whole scheme of chapter 7, the dating of chapter 9 by the reign of Darius, and the reference to Darius in 11:1 must all be called into question); (b) assigning to Cyrus only three (or four) successors when he had ten; (c) getting the chronology of the Persian period wrong, as in chapter 9; (d) going astray at the end of the "story", in describing the third Egyptian campaign leading up to the end, which never happened?

Or again, we may ask, what would be the point of revealing to someone in 6th-century Babylon a detailed account of the history of 2nd-century Palestine, an account which was to be kept secret until "the end"? Would it be anything more than a conjuring trick? Another question must be put alongside this one: can one imagine a succession of people — at least eight would be necessary, perhaps as many as sixteen, or more — handing down over four centuries a book none of them had read? If this is considered a realistic proposition, another question must also be considered: when the "time of the end" came, how would the current custodian of the sealed book know that it was time to open it?

To add a further question, with the objective of returning to firm ground: is there any compelling reason to suppose that any part of the book of Daniel was written by Daniel? Is it not more reasonable to conclude that it was written shortly before its publication, that is to say, probably soon after the events of December 167? Such a theory would account for the historical errors in respect of the earlier period; the lack of knowledge about the Persians and their chronology; the familiarity with Seleucid history. It would also account for the book's own insistence on its being "sealed" until the time of the end.

A purpose for the book in this period is not hard to find. In a time of political upheaval and religious persecution, a time when the Maccabaean rebellion — the first armed uprising of the people of Judah against their overlords for centuries past — was getting under way, the message of the book of Daniel was one of encouragement. To someone living in, say, 166 or 165 B.C., who recognized in the "little horn" or the "invading prince" the Seleucid overlord Antiochus IV, all the visions said, "This man has over-reached himself. In a couple of years it will all be over. The angels are on your side. The

Jewish people will be vindicated and God's kingdom established on earth. You can be sure of this because this was all revealed to Daniel in Babylon centuries ago. Hold on, fight on, you're going to win".

The stories too, as distinct from the visions, have a contribution to make. The stories fall into two groups: one kind, chapter 4 and chapter 5, says simply that God can easily dispose of the most powerful rulers and, by implication, he will deal with Antiochus, while the other kind, the stories of the furnace and the lion's den, offer encouragement to people persecuted on religious grounds. II Macc. 6ff have stories of persecutions under Antiochus and it is hardly without significance that Mattathias the father of Judas the Maccabee, refers in his last speech, I Macc. 2:49-64, to the incidents of Daniel in the lions' den and the three men in the furnace. Thus, both kinds of story have something to say to the Jews of *ca.* 165 B.C.

But is that all there is to be said? Was the whole book written, more or less overnight, with the intention of comforting and sustaining the people in their predicament? I think not, because one of our earliest observations was that the book falls into two parts (ignoring, for the moment, chapters 13 and 14). The visions have their function in the crisis of 167 and the following years — indeed they are said in the book to be addressed to the time of the end; these we may conceive of as having been written specially for those circumstances. The stories too, have a value in these circumstances but there are elements in them which suggest that they were not custom-made for those times. The most significant element lies in the representation of the various rulers, Nebuchadnezzar, Belshazzar, Darius, and of Daniel's relations with them. If the stories were composed for the purpose of giving encouragement to the Jews under the persecutions of Antiochus, we would expect all the rulers — whatever their names — to be Antiochus in disguise, but they are not. They are all apparently well-disposed towards their Jewish minister; they accept his Jewishness without fuss; when Darius is trapped into throwing Daniel to the lions he is distraught (similarly, in chapter 3, it is not Nebuchadnezzar who persecutes Daniel's friends but their colleagues who denounce them). All three rulers acknowledge Daniel's god to be the supreme God; there is no veiled prototype of Antiochus here. This factor alone might point towards the conclusion that the stories about Daniel and his friends are not part of the "propaganda-book" of the visions but previously existing stories which have been attached to it because they are capable of bearing suitable messages.

Can we go any further with the idea that the stories had a previous, independent existence? Is there anything in the book which will substantiate this notion? Early in our study we observed that there is a conflict between chapters 1 and 2 in relation to the chronological information contained in them, and this would appear to indicate that those two stories once existed independently of one another. We also noticed a conflict between chapter 1 and chapter 13, which might point to a similar conclusion but, since chapter 13 is one of the two chapters which do not occur in the Hebrew-Aramaic version of Daniel it is possible that this conflict is to be explained by the postulation of a separate origin for this part of the book.

The question implied by the existence of two different forms of the book of Daniel was the very first question raised in our study. It is now time to tackle that question.

Starting from first principles, there would appear to be two logical possibilities: either chapters 13 and 14, and the "extra" material in chapter 3 were added at some time to the older 12-chapter book, or the longer version is the original one and these passages have been evicted from the Hebrew-Aramaic version. We may approach the problem of choosing between these two possibilities by examining some of their implications[1].

If we assume, for a moment, that an original 12-chapter book was supplemented by extra material we must ask when and why this should have been done and where the supplementary material came from. In reply, we must say that the supposed additions do not add very much to the book, being simply a couple of stories about Daniel. It is hard to envisage these as having been specially composed for the purpose of being attached to the rest of the book. They do not round off the story — if Daniel's death were reported, for example, we could find some point in their composition, but as things stand it is hard to see them as having been specially written to supplement the shorter book. If they were not written for the purpose of supplementing the book, does it follow that they must have been part of the book from the beginning?

Let us now examine the other possibility. The question here is, if the original form of the book was the long one, when and why would chapters 13 and 14 have been dropped? The "why" is relatively easy to answer. In our survey of Dan. 1-12 we have found that every chapter has a message of hope and encouragement for the Jews in the persecutions of the 160s B.C. Not so chapters 13 and 14. A reason for dropping these chapters has thus been found, but the question "when" leads us into difficulties. Have we not concluded that the 12-chapter book was compiled in and for the time of the persecutions? How, then, could chapters 13 and 14 have been dropped from a book which was by implication non-existent? We are thrown back, it seems, to the first possibility, which we have already found unsatisfactory.

We began with two logical possibilities, neither of which seems satisfactory, so where do we go from here? Chapters 1-12 form a coherent block, which has a unity of purpose not shared by 13 and 14, therefore 13 and 14 must have been added, but 13 and 14 cannot be held to have been composed specially to supplement chapters 1-12, therefore they must have had an existence prior to their inclusion in Daniel.

The fact of the two different forms of the book of Daniel is best explained by the supposition that there was in the first place, i.e. well before the time that we have concluded that the "book of Daniel" came into existence, already a pool of stories, which existed independently of one another, about a Jew called Daniel who lived in Babylon in the time of the Babylonian and Persian empires and who was renowned for his God-given wisdom. In the 160s B.C. the compiler of the 12-chapter book of Daniel took over some of these stories, perhaps modifying them to make them bear a message for his own time, and used them as a launching pad for his own composition of encouragement/propaganda which he presented in the form of visions experienced by the hero of the stories. Other stories about Daniel, amongst which we may number the stories now found in Dan. 13 and 14, and perhaps also those of which fragments have been found at Qumran, he did not use because they did not lend themselves and could not easily be modified in such a way as to lend themselves to his purpose. However, once the 12-chapter book became detached in terms both of time and space from the environment in and for which it was created, the stories of Susanna and of Bel and the Dragon, doubtless well-established traditional tales involving the hero Daniel, could have been attached without compunction to the shorter book.

As a theory this is quite satisfactory. It seems to be the only possible explanation for the phenomenon of the two forms of the book. But how much evidence is there to support it? We have already found indications that different sections, even different chapters, of the book had different origins, but what about the suggestion that the individual stories had a history of their own, that they were modified by the compiler of the 12-chapter book in the process of their being incorporated into his composition? The clearest evidence of this having happened may be found in Dan. 2, where, in addition to the question raised by the date of the incident reported there, with which we have already dealt, two sets of questions are found to arise, both of which are best answered by the thesis that the chapter has undergone certain changes. The two sets of questions revolve around (i) Daniel and his part in the story, and (ii) the king and his dream.

(i) Daniel was, apparently, not present with the wise men at the first stage, when they were challenged to tell the king what his dream was. This, in itself, may be taken as further evidence that the story did not originate as a sequel to that in chapter 1, for, if Daniel had already proved himself to be ten times better than anybody else he really ought to have been called in on such an important job. His first appearance in chapter 2 comes at the point where he and his friends are being rounded up for execution along with the rest of the wise men (v.13). In this context it is demonstrated that Daniel had not been involved in the first place: he asks the executioner what is going on (v.15).

Having learnt from Arioch what is afoot, Daniel goes to the king and undertakes to bring him the solution to the problem by a specified time (v.16). Yet, after his prayer has been answered, he does not immediately carry out this promise. He goes first to Arioch, tells him not to kill the wise men and asks to be taken to the king. But surely, one might think, Arioch would already have been instructed to hold off from executing anybody. And why does Daniel need him to introduce him to the king?

Now comes the strangest point of all. Although Daniel, the wise man, has already undertaken, in a personal interview with the king, to supply the information the king had demanded, he does not march in to the king's presence as a courtier returning to fulfil his promise. Instead he is introduced by the "chief butcher" and not as the wise man returning to fulfil his undertaking but as an anonymous, and ostensibly unknown, Jewish deportee.

This is all very odd. However, if in reading the story the passage vv. 13-23 is omitted, we find that all the oddities have disappeared, leaving a straightforward story in which Daniel is an obscure individual who, having heard about the king's decree and the incompetence of the wise men, and being able by means of divine revelation to supply the answer to the king's question, presents himself to Arioch for introduction to the king.

This story is quite clearly independent of that in chapter 1 and, so long as it existed by itself, in isolation from other stories about Daniel, was perfectly satisfactory. No matter if other stories had different explanations for Daniel's coming to the notice of Nebuchadnezzar. But incorporated into a collection and standing next to the story of chapter 1, in which Daniel had already become known to Nebuchadnezzar, it would not do. It required modification to make Daniel into one of Nebuchadnezzar's wise men, but one who had not been present at the beginning of the story. This is where, both literally and figuratively speaking, the passage vv. 13-23 comes in. That passage is designed simply to identify the unknown Daniel of the earlier story (that is, the earlier form of chapter 2) with the Daniel of chapter 1, and also to keep his friends, who will be needed for chapter 3, to the fore. (The last verse or two of chapter 2 should also be considered to be editorial material.)

(ii) The king and his dream. The questions here arise from tensions within and between the account of the dream and that of its interpretation as given in the book, and between these and the interpretation put upon the dream by exegesis and perhaps implied in the book itself. To start from the top, Nebuchadnezzar had a dream about a statue consisting of four tiers, each of a different metal, which was destroyed by a stone. The explanation, given in the book, is that this represents a succession of four kingdoms which gives way to a divinely established kingdom. The exegesis which we have adopted above, which is not given explicitly in the book but which, in the context of Daniel's visions, seems clearly to be implied, is that the kingdoms referred to are the Babylonian, Median, Persian and Hellenistic empires, and an expected Messianic kingdom.

Three problems arise from this. First, why should all this have been revealed to Nebuchadnezzar? Would it not seem intrinsically probable that, as in the case of Nebuchadnezzar's vision of chapter 4, which was fulfilled within a twelvemonth, or Belshazzar's experience with the writing on the wall, which was fulfilled on the spot, the dream of chapter 2 should have some relevance to Nebuchadnezzar himself?

The second problem lies in squaring the interpretation with the original dream. In the dream, the four metals represent four kingdoms. That is fair enough, but together the four metals constitute one image. What can the image, as such, represent? We may recall that the whole image is crushed by the stone which makes its impact on the feet, but each successive empire would destroy its predecessor leaving only the last to be crushed by the stone.

Thirdly, there is the tension within the interpretation given in Daniel. The explanation of the top tier of the statue is given thus: "You, O King . . . are the head of gold". Logically we should expect that the other tiers should represent further members of the same category, that is to say other rulers, but in the book these are identified as kingdoms.

All three problems may be resolved by the following explanation. In the first place, Nebuchadnezzar's dream was intended to refer *not* to a succession of four imperial powers but to a succession of four individual rulers (the word kingdom could be understood as the domain or status of an individual ruler, so no change in the text need be postulated). If Nebuchadnezzar is taken to be the golden head, as it says in the text, the other three tiers of the statue would be his successors, Amel-marduk, Neriglissar and Nabonidus (Labashi-marduk who was ousted by Nabonidus after a very short reign being

87

too insignificant to mention). The image as a whole would thus be the neo-Babylonian empire from Nebuchadnezzar onwards and the stone, the divine instrument which smashed the image, would be Cyrus, who, in conquering the last king, Nabonidus, destroyed Babylonian power, and who, significantly, is described in Isa. 45 as Yahweh's Messiah. And, of course, the dream now has some significance for Nebuchadnezzar, inasmuch as it predicts the destruction of his great empire three generations later.

Understood in this way the story may, without the postulation of any supernatural element, be traced to an early date. Clearly it could have originated in the time of Cyrus, or even in that of Nabonidus; at any time after 550 B.C. it would not have required any abnormal ability to see that it was only a question of time before Cyrus would turn on Babylon and subdue it as he was subduing its neighbouring territories. We may note, at this point, that there is very little in Dan. 2 which does not fit with this explanation. Those few elements which led us at an earlier stage of our study happily to accept the four empire plus messianic kingdom interpretation — the description of the fourth kingdom as being as strong as iron, whereas no significance is attached to the particular metals used to symbolize the other kingdoms, the reference to the unstable mixture of iron and clay and to intermarriage, which may allude either to Alexander's policy of intermarriage or to the marriage alliances of the Seleucids and Ptolemies — may easily be seen as having been introduced by the person we have begun to identify as the compiler of Daniel.

To this compiler of Daniel, around 165 B.C., the story of Nebuchadnezzar's dream with its scheme of four rulers was a gift. With a little modification, which was not really necessary but helped to make his point clear, it could present the same picture as his own composition, the vision of chapter 7, which pointed forward to the Messianic/Jewish state. It might even be suggested that he obtained the idea from the older story, but before we proceed further along this path, it may be useful here to gather up some stray threads which were left loose at earlier stages.

When we examined the history of "Daniel's times" we focussed our attention on the errors and inaccuracies which we found in the book. That was the way the path led. But there are also various bits of accurate historical data to be found in Daniel, and that is worthy of mention. Among these are the fact that Nebuchadnezzar was responsible for the building of the splendid city of Babylon (4:30), that Cyrus was the successor of Astyages (14:1, although the wording of the passage may imply that the manner of the succession was not remembered) and, perhaps most notable, the preservation of the name of Belshazzar, which was unknown to historians in the classical period and was rediscovered only a little over a century ago. That such historical data are contained in them is in keeping with our judgement that the stories are quite old.

In addition to accurate details there are some curious elements, chief of these being the fact that the age of Darius, at the time of his conquest of Babylon, is given as 62. What is odd about this statement is that Cyrus, who in reality conquered Babylon at the time when, according to Daniel, Darius is represented as doing so, would have been about 62 years old at that time. Thus, the statement in Daniel calls for some comment or, if possible, explanation, but first a word must be said about the historical inaccuracies. There were two of these: the dating of Daniel's capture in the third year of Jehoiakim, and the person of Darius. Having offered explanations for other historical errors (the successors of Cyrus, the chronology of the Persian period) are we simply to dismiss these matters as either inexplicable or of no consequence?

The reference to the third year of Jehoiakim is explicable on the supposition that the compiler of Daniel himself wrote chapter 1 as an introduction to his complete work. The suggestion is plausible inasmuch as the chapter contains nothing very exciting. It may be hard to envisage it as ever having existed as a story in its own right, but it does have a relevance to the situation of the 160s when the Jews were being forced to eat pagan food. But whether or not he composed the story, it may be suggested that he supplied the date in 1:1, having "found" it in II Kings 24:1, where reference is made to Jehoiakim's having served Nebuchadnezzar for three years. That these were not his first three years is not clear from that passage, and someone looking for a date for Nebuchadnezzar's first involvement in Judah might well conclude that it was in the third year of Jehoiakim.

What about Darius? One thing we are told about him in Daniel is that he introduced administrative reforms, appointing 120 satraps to govern his empire. Now, as it happens, there was a Darius (there were three of them in all, this is Darius I) who instituted reforms of this kind and, in the process, gave the Persian empire its definitive shape, although the total number of satraps was 20. This Darius, incidentally, "conquered" Babylon at the beginning of his reign (522-486) when he put down a rebellion there. It is possible that this was the Darius of the Daniel in the lion's den story, in the original form of that story, and that this original story goes well back into history. If so, there would be a problem when the story was integrated with the others in the book of Daniel, in that Daniel would have been very old in the time of Darius I if he had been captured before 600 B.C. The compiler of Daniel, in the 160s B.C. might, however, not have realized that; it would certainly not be safe to assume that he would.

To complete our explanation of Darius the Mede, and also to bring our study of Daniel to its conclusion, let us return to chapter 2.

The story in chapter 2 is the foundation stone of the whole book, and the key to understanding its compilation. That story, one of several which had existed for some considerable time, had a scheme of four successive kings giving way to a fifth, motivated by divine power. Our author, living in the mid-second century and looking for an imminent Messianic state, applied that scheme to a longer timescale than had originally been intended. If the culmination of the scheme was to be in his own time, the fourth power had to be the Hellenistic empires, and so, if the first was to be the Babylonian, as it had to be, he needed to find two powers to bridge the gap. He knew of the duality "the Medes and the Persians", he knew of the historical relationship between them (this is displayed in chapter 8) and he certainly knew that prophets had looked for the destruction of Babylon by Medes (Is. 13:17; Jer. 51:11,28) and so he developed his four empire picture, with the Medes succeeding the Babylonians and preceding the Persians.

Next, in order to indicate to his readers, who would not know as much history as he did, what was going on, he needed to have Daniel live under Babylonian, Median, and Persian rule, so that only one empire would be left to Daniel's "future". He had stories in which Babylonian and Persian rulers were mentioned, but there were none involving Median rulers, because he had just invented the Median empire, and so he made Darius a Mede (perhaps, though more probably not, recognising the historical problem which would be created by keeping him a Persian) and was thus able to date the visions of Daniel by Babylonian, Median and Persian rulers. As a part of this process, Darius's name had to be inserted at the end of Dan. 5, where previously, in the old story, the name of Cyrus must have stood. Cyrus's age was there too, and there was no reason to excise it, so there it still stands, giving rise to the curious situation we have noted.

It is time now to draw our study to its close. We set out to answer the question, "What is the book of Daniel?", and we may say: The book of Daniel is a book compiled *ca.* 165 B.C. for the purpose of giving encouragement to the Jews in a period of persecution. It looks for an imminent end to the contemporary situation, for the triumph of the Jews and the establishment of an age of enduring peace and righteousness. Chapters 7-12 were written for this purpose at that time. Cast in the form of visions experienced by Daniel, this gives authority to its statements. Daniel was probably already well-known to the original audience of the book (*cf.* Mattathias in I Macc. 2) from stories which had existed for centuries past. The compiler utilized

several of these stories as an introduction to his own work —
including one which, by a remarkable stroke of luck, suited his own
purpose very nicely — indeed it probably gave him the idea. Thus, the
12-chapter book was produced. The 14-chapter book came about
through the addition of a couple of stories which the "compiler" had
not included, but which in another environment seemed, quite
properly in one sense, to belong naturally with the rest of the stories
about Daniel.

A final note may be added, in conformity with the first part of this
book, to show that the statement of Eccles. 1:9 applies to biblical
studies as to much else. The suggestion that the book of Daniel was
written in the second century B.C. does not solely result from modern
study; it was made already in the third century of our era.

Notes

1 The discussion will focus on the stories of Susanna and of Bel and the Dragon,
   which may be isolated with relative ease. With the "additions" to chapter 3,
   however, we are in a different situation because these are integrated with the rest of
   the chapter. The question here is one of deciding which of the two forms of chapter
   3 is likely to be the older, which is a more complex question than that of the
   relationship between the 12-chapter and 14-chapter books.

EPILOGUE AND PROSPECT

Epilogue and Prospect

What we have done in our study of the book of Daniel has been to lay down a method for the pursuit of our investigation and to pursue this investigation, according to that method, to a point at which it is possible to give an answer to the question, "What is the book of Daniel?". That the answers arrived at, at any stage of the investigation, are not necessarily the only, or even the best, answers is entirely possible, for such is the nature of scholarship. But if the reader is prompted to pursue matters further for himself, the book will have served its purpose.

Although we have drawn our study to a conclusion, it is in reality far from finished. Many things remain undone, questions unasked and unanswered. Many matters of detail within the book remain unexamined; the vexed question of why the book should have been written in two languages (Hebrew from 1:1 to 2:4a, and again from 8:1 to 12:13; Aramaic in the intervening section) has not even been opened; nor has the question of the relationship of the book with other writings, in the Bible or outside it. Judgement has been suspended on the question of the two forms of chapter 3 and, while the suggestion has been made that the book is, at least in part, a collection of older, originally independent stories, no attempt has been made, except in a limited way for chapter 2, to investigate the origin and development of these stories.

Such matters have been discussed in recent scholarly literature. For a clear presentation of the major issues and an assessment of the most recent scholarship on Daniel, see P.R. Davies, *Daniel* (Old Testament Guides, 4), Sheffield 1985.

APPENDICES

Appendix 1: **Contents of the Jewish Bible**

A.   Torah

(Divided into 5 sections, named after 1st word in each and given names in (Greek) translation)

(i)	*B'reshit*	(In the beginning)	:	Genesis
(ii)	*Sh'mot*	(Names)	:	Exodus
(iii)	*Vayikra*	(He called)	:	Leviticus
(iv)	*B'midbar*	(In the wilderness)	:	Numbers
(v)	*D'varim*	(Words)	:	Deuteronomy

B.   Prophets

(a)   Former Prophets:

(i)   Joshua
(ii)   Judges
(iii)   Samuel, I & II
(iv)   Kings, I & II

(b)   Latter Prophets:

(i)   Isaiah
(ii)   Jeremiah
(iii)   Ezekiel
(iv)   The Twelve (i.e. Hosea, Joel, Amos, Obadiah, Jonah, Micah, Nahum, Habakkuk, Zephaniah, Haggai, Zechariah, Malachi.)

C.   Writings

(i)   Psalms
(ii)   Proverbs
(iii)   Job
(iv)   Song of Songs
(v)   Ruth
(vi)   Lamentations
(vii)   Ecclesiastes
(viii)   Esther
(ix)   Daniel
(x)   Ezra-Nehemiah
(xi)   Chronicles, I & II

Appendix 2: **Contents of the Protestant Old Testament**

A. **Law***

Genesis
Exodus
Leviticus
Numbers
Deuteronomy

B. **History***

Joshua
Judges
Ruth
I Samuel
II Samuel
I Kings
II Kings
I Chronicles
II Chronicles
Ezra
Nehemiah
Esther   [*10 chapters*]

C. **Poetry***

Job
Psalms
Proverbs
Ecclesiastes
Song of Songs

D. **Prophecy***

Isaiah
Jeremiah
Lamentations
Ezekiel
Daniel   [*12 chapters*]
Hosea
Joel
Amos
Obadiah
Jonah
Micah
Nahum
Habakkuk
Zephaniah
Haggai
Zechariah
Malachi

*   These headings are not normally printed in Christian bibles.

Appendix 3: **Contents of the Roman Catholic Old Testament**

A. **Law**

Genesis
Exodus
Leviticus
Numbers
Deuteronomy

B. **History**

Joshua (Josue)[1]
Judges
Ruth
I Samuel (I Kings)
II Samuel (II Kings)
I Kings (III Kings)
II Kings (IV Kings)
I Chronicles (I Paralipomenon)
II Chronicles (II Paralipomenon)
Ezra (I Esdras)
Nehemiah (II Esdras)
Tobit (Tobias)
Judith
Esther [*16 chapters*]
I Maccabees (I Machabees)[2]
II Maccabees (II Machabees)

C. **Poetry**

Job
Psalms
Proverbs
Ecclesiastes
Song of Songs (Canticle of Canticles)
Wisdom
Ecclesiasticus

D. **Prophecy**

Isaiah (Isaias)
Jeremiah (Jeremias)
Lamentations
Baruch
Ezekiel (Ezechiel)
Daniel [*14 chapters*]
Hosea (Osee)
Joel
Amos
Obadiah (Abdias)
Jonah (Jonas)
Micah (Micheas)
Nahum
Habakkuk (Habacuc)
Zephaniah (Sophonias)
Haggai (Aggeus)
Zechariah (Zachirias)
Malachi (Malachias)

[1]   The titles in brackets are used in translations made from the Latin Vulgate.

[2]   The books of Maccabees are sometimes placed after the prophetic books as the latest books of the Old Testament.

Appendix 4: **Contents of the Orthodox Old Testament**

A. **Law**

Genesis
Exodus
Leviticus
Numbers
Deuteronomy

B. **History**

Joshua
Judges
Ruth
I Samuel
II Samuel
I Kings
II Kings
I Chronicles
II Chronicles
I Esdras
II Esdras (= Ezra-Nehemiah)
Tobit
Judith
Esther   [*16 chapters*]
I Maccabees
II Maccabees
III Maccabees

C. **Poetry**

Job
Psalms   [*151 chapters*]
Prayer of Manasseh
Proverbs
Ecclesiastes
Song of Songs
Wisdom
Ecclesiasticus

D. **Prophecy**

Isaiah
Jeremiah
Lamentations
Baruch
Ezekiel
Daniel   [*14 chapters*]
Hosea
Joel
Amos
Obadiah
Jonah
Micah
Nahum
Habakkuk
Zephaniah
Haggai
Zechariah
Malachi

INDEX

Index of Texts

(a) Bible

Genesis
1:1	21
4:8	36
6:19f	28
7:7-10	28
7:8-9	28
7:11-13	28
7:16	28
12:6	11,12
12:8	26
12:10-20	27
15:2	26
14:14	15
17	27
18	27
20:1-18	27
22:14	11
26:1-11	27
32:28	27
35:10	27
36:31	15
36:31-39	17
37	28ff
39:1	28
47:31	38

Exodus
3:6	22
6:2,3	25,26
16:35	15
24:4	11,21

Leviticus
24:16	23

Numbers
12:3	14
21:14	13,25
22-24	10
33:2	11,21

34:10	14
34:27f	21

Deuteronomy
1:1	14
3:11	12
11-27	13
31:9	11,13,21
34:6	12
34:12	21

Joshua
5:12	15
8:31	20,21
10	25
23:6	20
24	10

Judges
18:29	15
18:30	13

I Samuel
3:13	34
13:1	33
14:41	36f
17	5
25	8

II Samuel
1	25
7	23
12	23
21	5
22	35
24	23

I Kings
2:3	20

II Kings
14:6   20,21
14:25   15
16:6   39
17   16
22   16,19
22:8   13
23:1ff   13
24:1   89

Isaiah
2:2-4   5
13:17   90
45:1   79,88

Jeremiah
25   71
25:1   59f
25:11ff   69
29   71
29:10   69
36   8
46:2   60
51:11,28   90

Amos
6:12   38

Micah
4:1-3   5

Psalms
18   35
78   17
126   13
137   13

Proverbs
1:1   9,13
10:1   9,13
25:1   9
30:1   9,13
31:1   9,13

Job
7:20   34

Song of Songs
1:1   9

Ecclesiastes
1:1   9
1:9   91

Daniel
1-6   50f,53
1   44,53,83f
1:1   58ff,89
1:5   49
1:18f   49
1:21   50,53
2   44,53,56,65ff,83,85ff,90
2:1   54
2:13   49,86
2:15   86
2:16   50,86
2:18   49
2:25   49,54
2:37f   65,68
2:43   68
3   45,83f,91
4   45,56,83,87
4:30   88
5   45,51,83,90
5:10ff   50,53
6   45,51,62
6:29   50
7-12   15,50f,53,55f,65f,90
7   46,51,55,66ff,72,82
7:7   67f
7:19   68
7:24   66
7:25   66,72
8   46,51,66ff,70,72
8:3   69
8:11   73
8:14   67,71
8:20   69

8:26	55	11:31	73
9	46,69ff,72,76,78f,82	11:34	76
9:1	63f	11:37	75
9:13	20	11:44	76
9:24	70	11:45	76
9:25	70f	12	51
9:26	70,72f	12:1	76
9:27	71,79	12:4	55f
10-12	46,55f,71f	12:9	55f
10:1	46,50,53,72	12:13	50
11	78	13-14	50f
11:1	62f,82	13	46,51,53,84f
11:2	72,76	14	46,51,84f
11:3	72	14:1	88
11:4	72		
11:5-20	73	Ezra	
11:5	74	3:2	20
11:6	73f	6:18	20,21
11:7	74		
11:8	74	Nehemiah	
11:10	73f	8:1	20
11:11	74	8:14-15	21
11:13	74	13:1	20,21
11;16	74		
11:18	74	I Chronicles	
11:20	73f	29:29	22
11:21	73,75		
11:25	75	II Chronicles	
11:29	75	23:18	20
11:30-39	76	25:4	20,21
11:30	75	35:12	20

(b)   Apocrypha

II (IV) Esdras		2	90
14	14	2:49-64	83
		6	76
I Maccabees			
1	75		
1:41ff	75	II Maccabees	
1:54	76	6ff	83

(c) New Testament

Mark		Hebrews	
12:26	21	11:21	38
Luke		Jude	
20:37	21	14,15	4

(d) Talmud

Baba Bathra
14b-15a   8

Index of Authors

Astruc, Jean	18ff, 25	Josephus	61,80
Clements, R.E.	23	Millard, A.	59,64
Davies, P.R.	95	Newton, Sir Isaac	15ff
de Wette, W.M.L.	19	Porteous, N.	64
Eichhorn, J.G.	19	Rast, W.E.	23
Ewald, H.	19	Rowley, H.H.	64
Geddes, A.	19	Spinoza, Baruch	14f
Graf, K.H.	19	Tucker, G.M.	23
Grotius, H.	62	Weingreen, J.	40
Habel, N	40	Wellhausen, J.	19
Herodotus	62	Whitcomb, J.C.	63f
Hobbes, Thomas	12ff	Wiseman, D.J.	63f
ibn Ezra, Abraham	11f,15	Xenophon	62